## CONTENTS

CONSTITUTION FOR THE BAPTIST
   BROTHERHOOD UNION.............................3
LIFE OF CHRIST................................9- 42
ONE YEAR'S STUDY ON MAN FOR
   THE BROTHERHOOD..........................43-70
THE HOLY SPIRIT..............................72- 87
CHRISTIAN GIVING AND
   PAYING TITHES.............................89-104

# CONSTITUTION

## FOR THE

## BAPTIST BROTHERHOOD UNION

### By

### REV. S. A. PLEASANTS, JR.

1983
**Reprinted 2018**
Published by
R.H. BOYD PUBLISHING CORPORATION
6717 Centennial Blvd. • Nashville, Tennessee 37209-1049
R. H. Boyd, Founder
LaDonna Boyd, President and CEO

## CONSTITUTION

### By: Rev. S. A. Pleasants, Jr.

Motto: All men in the lead in the Church, now, and forever; leading for Jesus according to His Word and Spirit only.

Second Motto: Teach the Word in the home, with a consecrated heart, following in the footsteps of the Saviour, leading all men to God.

We, the laymen of the church of Jesus Christ, in order to carry out the will of our heavenly Father, by making His word and Spirit, our daily Guide, do ordain and establish this Constitution for the laymen of His Church.

### ARTICLE I.—Name.

This organization shall be known as the Brotherhood Union of the Church of Christ Jesus, worshiping at _____ .

Many call this organization, "League" "Movement," etc. I prefer Union after the Bible term. —Psalm 13:1—(You may use yours).

### ARTICLE II.—Object.

Its object shall be to harness every layman, junior and senior in the Church for His special use; that His Church might take the lead in every thing in the time world.

### ARTICLE III.—Membership.

Its membership shall be any and all laymen, junior and senior, who are members of the church of Christ Jesus.

### ARTICLE IV.—Officers.

Its officers shall be a President, First and Second Vice-President, Secretary, First and Second Assistant Secretary, Treasurer, Corresponding Secretary, Musical Director, Sunshine Inspirer and a

Director for Juniors.

## ARTICLE V.—Duty of Officers.

**Section 1.—President.** It shall be the duty of the President to consult the Pastor on everything necessary before acting. Preside over all meetings, and keep the members in perfect harmony with the will and spirit of the Church of Christ Jesus.

**Section 2.—The Vice-Presidents.** They shall act in the absence of the President, or upon his request or the request of the body.

**Section 3.—The Secretary.** He shall keep the records as perfect as possible of all the proceedings of the Union, making his report weekly, monthly, quarterly and annually when required.

**Section 4.—The Assistant Secretaries.** They shall act in the absence of the Secretary or upon his or the Union's request.

**Section 5.—The Treasurer.** He shall take charge of the money, and report same to the Financial Secretary of the church at each meeting.

**Section 6.—Corresponding Secretary.** He shall do all of the corresponding for the Union.

**Section 7.—Musical Director.** He shall have charge of all music, selecting and directing same.

**Section 8.—Sunshine Inspirer.** He shall bring or cause to be brought 3 or 5 minute lectures at the end of each meeting, on inspirational sunshine.

**Section 9.—Junior Director.** He shall assist the President in organizing the Juniors, and direct them in their work, being subject to the President and General Body.

## ARTICLE VI.—Committees

Committees shall be as follows:

- Praying Band
- Soul-Saving
- Uplift
- Weary Travelers

Finance
Education
Missionary
Fellowship
Life Keepers
Program

## ARTICLE VII.—Duties of Committees.

**Section 1.—Praying Band.** It shall cause the Union and the Church to conduct regular prayer meetings. It shall pray in the homes and anywhere the Holy Spirit may direct; for the salvation of the lost throughout the world, and the development of the Church.

**Section 2.—Soul-Saving.** It shall constantly plan, and labor for the salvation of souls wherever sinners are to be found, regardless of race or color, and cause the Union and Church to save souls daily.

**Section 3.—Uplift.** It shall seek all who are down in the slums and the underworld, in mind, and in body, and lift them up to heights of truth and righteousness for the Kingdom of our Father.

**Section 4.—Weary Travelers.** It shall seek those who have started in the services of our Father and become discouraged because of various reasons and bring them back into usefulness in the Union and Church.

**Section 5.—Finance.** It shall manage the financial side of the Union and the Church, so as to keep the spirit of paying and giving ever alive in the church as is taught in the Bible.

**Section 6.—Education.** It shall see that the members of the Union and Church are religiously educated, and select or cause to be selected the proper literature for them, making the Bible the only Book to be the Guide of the Union and Church.

**Section 7.—Missionary.** It shall establish or cause to be established in every home in the church and community a family altar; go or cause to go into any place far or near, any or all of its members for any righteous cause, and help relieve any condition necessary, natural or spiritual.

**Section 8.—Fellowship.** It shall see to it that perfect peace is kept in the Union and Church; that funds are provided for the needy who attend the Union and Church, and that others are made happy in or out of the Church. Provide for the social side of the Union and Church by helping those appointed to do so.

**Section 9.—Life Keepers.** They shall push forward all of the work of the Union and Church, cause everything to function as organized in the Union and Church; and shall publish or cause to be published all matters of publicity, for the Union and the Church.

**Section 10.—Program.** The Program Committee shall make the programs for the Union and help make the programs for any auxiliary of the Church proper, when called upon. All of the elected officers of the Union and the chairman of each committee shall constitute the Program Committee.

### ARTICLE VIII.—Change In Name.

Each committee, when functioning during the week, and when reporting its work, shall be called committee; but when in its teaching and training service preparing for its work, it shall be called a class.

### ARTICLE IX.—The Governing Body.

The Union must be subject to the pastor and church in everything. When it ceases to be governed by the Pastor and Church, it must cease to function with its present officers. The Church and Pastor then may organize another with newly elected officers, who will obey the Pastor and Church. As holds good with the Union itself, the same is applied to any subordinate member or officer of the Union.

### ARTICLE X.—Teachers In And For The Union.

Each class shall select from its own committee, teachers for itself, letting as many be teachers for the class as have the ability to do so, teaching interchangeably as the class sees it. Using this method, it gives the class a thoroughly prepared teaching group in the course of time.

# THE LIFE OF CHRIST

## A TREATISE ON THE LIFE OF THE SAVIOR

### IN WEEKLY LESSONS FOR THE BROTHERHOOD UNION

By

**REV. A. A. PLEASANTS, JR.**

1—Introduction.
2—His Existence As God.
3—The Turning Point In His Life.
4—Christ Jesus The God-man

---

Scriptures for devotions must be taken from each weekly lesson. Where there are many scriptures given, the leader of devotions will select the one dictated by the Holy Spirit.

## 1ST WEEK

## CHRIST JESUS

### Introduction

After having studied man one year in order that the laymen might rightly take his place in the church, and fill it well until death, we now come to the greatest subject that is known to him. When this is prayerfully and carefully studied and made into the mind, heart, spirit and body of man, a new day will dawn in the church and the world. When the human man will in his spirit study The Divine Man, he will let the Holy Spirit completely change his whole being. The Subject, "Christ Jesus" the greatest of all, is the one that claims our attention in this study. Definition of the subject. Christ means "the anointed One." Jesus means "Savior of the world." Christ Jesus means "the anointed Saviour of the world" (Matthew 1:21). He is the only standard for man. Each life lived must be like His if accepted by our Father. For this to be done man must surrender all to Him to begin with. He must be lived over in the world in order that He might save the world, and this life must be lived by each layman as well as the Preacher. Ever keep in mind, that His life gives life to all.

## 2ND WEEK

## HIS EXISTENCE AS GOD

He existed as God before He became man. **In the beginning was the Word, and the Word was with God, and the word was God** (John 1:1). As God, He had no beginning. He is equal to the Father in all of His attributes. I and the Father are one, (John 10:30). When laymen receive this study of the Christ, they will take their places in the church without fail. Because the Christ filled His place in everything, being God, He is Eternal, that which is Eternal is God. The life was manifested, and we have seen, and bear witness and declare unto you the life, the Eternal life, which was with the

# THE LIFE OF CHRIST

Father and was manifested unto us (John 1:2). Being Eternal as the Father, He makes all He lives in Eternal. I give unto them eternal life; and they shall never perish (John 10:28).

## 3RD WEEK
### HIS EXISTENCE AS GOD (Cont.)

Being with the Father, and being God, all things that came into being were created by Him. All things came into being through Him, and apart from Him nothing that now exists came into being (John 1:2).

Had He not been God He could not have created all things, because God is the only Creator. You may search all beings that exist and you cannot find in any of them a creator.

All the intelligent beings we have a knowledge of, are mankind, angels and the Deity. Our thorough knowledge of things tell us that in all of these there is no one who creates but the Deity. All men know that they are not creators. No angel has ever been known to create anything, and will never be known to do so. Hence God, as Father, Son, and Holy Spirit, is Creator of all things, and since He as God created all things, He as God keeps all things in existence.

## 4TH WEEK
### HIS EXISTENCE AS GOD (Cont.)

Christ as God has all the glory which the Father had, until He divested Himself of it to become man's Redeemer. **And now, Father, glorify thou me with thine own self with the glory which I had with thee before the world was** (John 17:5). To have such glory before the world was, He had to be God. We have no knowledge of any one existing before the creation of things but God, and inasmuch as He existed before the world was, He is God.

He was not brought into existence somewhere down the line of our Father's creation, but helped to begin, carry on and complete all things that were created, All life was in Him as Creator of the universe.

In him was life; and the life was the light of men (John 1:4). For Him to have all life in Himself makes Him truly God. We know of none who has all life in Himself but the Deity. To know Him as such is the basis of the new spiritual life which God invites us to share with Him.

## 5TH WEEK

### HIS EXISTENCE AS GOD (Cont.)

Being God, He was in the beginning before heaven and earth were created. **The Word was with God** (John 1:1b). Heaven was not created for Him, but for men and angels. He did not need any heaven for His dwelling place, because He is more than heaven. In fact, heaven is in Him. This is true of Him as God the Eternal. **But will God indeed dwell on the earth? behold, the heaven and heaven of heavens cannot contain thee; how much less this house that I have builded?** (1 Kings 8:27). As God, He existed without a human body. He rightly taught while here that God is a Spirit: and they that worship him must worship him in spirit and in truth (John 4:24). He is just as much Spirit as the Father, and demonstrated it long before He became a man. He, as God, preached in the time of Noah to those who were lost in the flood while they lived. This He did in His Spirit as God (1 Peter 3:18-20).

## 6TH WEEK

### HIS EXISTENCE AS GOD (Cont.)

As God, He created man before He Himself became man. **And God said, Let us make man in our image, after our likeness** (Genesis 1:26a). This was not in human expression, but divine expressions given to us afterwards in human language. When this was expressed, there was not a single human being in existence. At this time, man existed only in the being of God. Since this is true, Christ Jesus had to be God, that He might enter into the conversation. As God, He was the image spoken of by the Father, Son and the Holy Spirit. We know that they are fully God. That image as singled out in other portions of this guide lets us know

# THE LIFE OF CHRIST

that he was fully God at that time without a human body. **After our likeness,** brings out the idea of the Deity, in the human flesh of Christ Jesus; who became fully human, yet in which all the Deity is fully seen (Hebrews 1:3).

## 7TH WEEK

### HIS EXISTENCE AS GOD (Cont.)

As God, He created man before He Himself became a man. **And God created man in His own image, in the image of God created He him; male and female created he them** (Genesis 1:27). The twenty-sixth verse tells the conversation as carried on by the Deity in contemplation. The twenty-seventh verse tells that the expression in the twenty-sixth verse was put into execution, and that the results of the twenty-sixth verse were realized in the twenty-seventh, in the creation of a full grown man as contemplated. The last part of the twenty-seventh verse brings out the idea that this man, created in the image of God, was the only one human seed made in the perfect image and likeness of God. Such a wonderful creation of man, not saying anything about all the other things created, should wake up the very best in every layman, to the end, that he will be delighted to again take the lead in the church of Christ Jesus, and never cease until Our Father shall have the victory over all humanity.

## 8TH WEEK

### HIS EXISTENCE AS GOD(Cont).

As God, He was in the council when it was said, **and let them have dominion over the fish of the sea, and over the fowl of the air, and over the cattle, and over all the earth, and over every creeping thing that creepeth upon the earth** (Genesis 1:26b).

Here we have the statement to grant to man power over the

earth, and everything in it, after his creation. "**Let them have dominion,**" expresses that power would be given to all human beings, that live upon earth after creation, to rule every thing, everywhere, for man's own pleasure, and God's own glory.

The above statement was made before man's creation. Our Father, Son and Holy Spirit set the example for man to always make preparation, using the best and all that are prepared to be in the council and plan all that is to be done. Much of man's failure comes because he does not plan well that which is to be done, by using the best spiritual thinkers living in the plan, so that the wisest council may be had, in order to produce the best results possible.

## 9TH WEEK

### HIS EXISTENCE AS GOD (Cont.)

As God, He took part in carrying out the statement made in the council before man's creation, expressed in the following scripture after man's creation. **And God blessed them, and God said unto them, Be fruitful, and multiply, and replenish the earth, and subdue it: and have dominion over the fish of the sea, and over the fowl of the air, and over every living thing that moveth upon the earth** (Genesis 1:28). The blessing gave to them the ability to be all He required of them to be, and to do all He required of them to do. A greater blessing cannot come to man than that of having the ability to be and to do all that His Creator requires. The greatest happiness that comes into man's soul is his ability to do the will of Our Father.

In this verse we have five things man is to do: (a) Be fruitful, (b) Multiply, (c) Fill the earth; (d) Subdue the earth, (e) Have dominion over every living thing. The word replenish in the Authorized version should have been translated 'Fill' as given in the Hebrew text. For all of the above to be done without defects, there had to be a race of mankind that was truly like the Deity. Man has failed in the commands given him, because he did not live up to the commands of His Creator.

## 10TH WEEK

### HIS EXISTENCE AS GOD (Cont.)

**Have dominion over the fish of the sea.** For this to be done, man must be able to handle the waters that the fish lived in. As God, Christ Jesus gave man some of the powers He Himself had when he was a man in human flesh. It was shown somewhat when He commanded Peter to come to Him walking on the water (Matthew 14:28-31). And it was shown in full, when the man Christ Jesus walked on the water Himself (Matthew 14:25, 26). Man in his first creation was a figure of Christ Jesus the man (Romans 5:14).

## 11TH WEEK

### HIS EXISTENCE AS GOD (Cont.)

**"Have dominion over every thing that moveth upon the earth."** As God, Christ Jesus gave him the greatest power, beyond that of all creatures, that moved upon the earth. Whenever He said to man do this or that, He gives him the ability to carry out His commands. The master beast of the forest obeyed him perfectly. The failure to master them now as then, comes because he fails to do now as then, because he has drifted into sin (Romans 3:23).

## 12TH WEEK

### HIS EXISTENCE AS GOD (Cont.)

As God, He walked and talked with Abraham (Genesis 18:16-21). As a faithful Son of his Father as God, He attended to all the business assigned Him. It was the delight of the Father, to have His Son attend to His business more than men, who delight to turn into the hands of their sons their business affairs.

When He said: **"This is my beloved Son in whom I am well pleased,"** He did not mean only for the present act, but for all He had done and would do, as God equal to Him. And just as He pleased Him in the righteous act of baptism, He had pleased Him in everything He had done as God, even before He was born in the human flesh.

As God, He educated Moses in Midian in all the things He wanted him to know, that he might lead the Israelites out of Egypt. At the close of the great religious school He kept Moses in, He as God appeared to him in the burning bush, and gave him the command to go into Egypt and deliver the people which He had brought into the world.

## 13TH WEEK

### HIS EXISTENCE AS GOD (Cont.)

As God, His existence in angelic form was temporary, but long enough to accomplish His purpose. During the ages before He became a man, He was often seen in angelic form. As God, He could not appear unto man as such, because man after having sinned could not see the face of God as such and live. Hence He made use of angelic forms.

The ancients called Him the Angel of the Lord, because of His form. Beginning in the book of Genesis are these expressions: "The Angel of the Lord, The Angel of Jehovah," etc. These are sprinkled all through the Bible and are especially noticeable in the Old Covenant (Genesis 22:11, 15-18; Isaiah 63:9; Zechariah 1:12).

Forms or bodies do not change His character. He is verily God. As such He remains through all the ages, in all conditions, under all circumstances. To study Him as such, in the spirit of His being, will make men become fixed in their souls, to take the God-appointed place in all of the activities of the Church, the body of Christ Jesus.

# THE LIFE OF CHRIST

## 14TH WEEK

### HIS EXISTENCE AS GOD (Cont.)

As God in angelic form, He talked to Habar in Abraham's time. And the Angel of Jehovah found her by a fountain of water in the wilderness, by the fountain in the way of Shur. And He said, **Hagar, Sarai's maid, whence camest thou? and whither wilt thou go? And she said, I flee from the face of my mistress Sarai. And the angel of the Lord said unto her, Return to thy mistress, and submit thyself under her hands. And the angel of the Lord said unto her, Behold, thou art with child, and shalt bear a son, and shalt call his name Ishmael; because the Lord hath heard thy affliction. And he will be a wild man; his hand will be against every man, and every man's hand against him; and he shall dwell in the presence of all his brethren. And she called the name of the Lord that spake unto her, Thou God seest me: for she said, Have I also here looked after him that seeth me?** (Genesis 16:7-13)?

The expressions of promise in the above statements give proof that the "Angel of Jehovah" is Christ Jesus as God. He is the only one that can multiply human seed so as to make it increase so no one can number them, verse 10 above. Hagar knew Him through His presence as God and said of Him **Thou art the God that seeth.**

## 15TH WEEK

### HIS EXISTENCE AS God (Cont.)

As God, He stayed with Moses and the Israelites all the time. All ate the same spiritual food and all drank the same spiritual drink; for they drank from the Spiritual Rock that went with them, and that Rock was Christ (1 Corinthians 10:3, 4).

He never left any that belonged to Our Father, but like a good Shepherd He attended them, protected them, and saw to it that all were safe in the fold of His Father. From the beginning of creation, He as God, had been with man and supplies all that Our Father has required of Him. That was one of the reasons that David said, **The Lord is my shepherd; I shall not want** (Psalm 23:1). **He made known his ways unto Moses,** his acts unto the children of Israel (Psalm 103:7).

That Israelitish crowd must confess in the judgment, that the One that they are judged by followed them from Egypt's bondage into the land of promise, and was their protection and guide all the way, and yet they did not obey Him.

## 16TH WEEK

### HIS EXISTENCE AS GOD (Cont.)

As God, He stood and talked with Joshua. **And it came to pass, when Joshua was by Jericho, that he lifted up his eyes and looked, and, behold, there stood a man over against him with his sword drawn in his hand: and Joshua went unto him, and said unto him, Art thou for us, or for our adversaries? And he said, Nay; but as captain of the host of the Lord am I now come. And Joshua fell on his face to the earth, and did worship, and said unto him, What saith my lord unto his servant? And the captain of the Lord's host said unto Joshua, Loose thy shoe from off thy foot; for the place whereon thou standest is holy. And Joshua did so** (Joshua 5:13-15).

He is the Angel of the Lord of the Old Covenant, that did the biddings of Our Father clothed in angelic form before He was wrapped in humanity. He as God had been in the form of angels and came to man, before He came to man in the form of man. As God, He is able to use any form, and anybody He wants, and not be hypocrital in any, because all are His, both men and angels.

# THE LIFE OF CHRIST

## 17TH WEEK

### HIS EXISTENCE AS GOD (Cont.)

As God, He was present in every place at the same time. **Whither shall I go from thy spirit? or whither shall I flee from thy presence? If I ascend up into heaven, thou art there: if I make my bed in hell, behold, thou art there. If I take the wings of the morning, and dwell in the uttermost parts of the sea; Even there shall thy hand lead me, and thy right hand shall hold me** (Psalm 139:7-10).

When laymen awake to the consciousness of the presence of Christ Jesus, as God they will conduct their lives so as to influence other men and women for good in all walks of life. It is not enough for Christ Jesus as God to have been present at every place at the same time, but those who were guided best and lived best, were fully aware of His presence. So it must be in our day and time. The man who keeps in mind that Christ Jesus, as God, is everywhere, and that His great ear hears all he says, and that His great eye sees all he does, will so conduct himself so as to influence men to come into His kingdom and take their places where they are so much needed.

## 18TH WEEK

### HIS EXISTENCE AS GOD (Cont.)

**Can any hide himself in secret places that I shall not see him? saith the Lord. Do not I fill heaven and earth? saith the Lord** (Jeremiah 23:24).

There were no secret places with Him, as God. Secret places are for men. Everything is as present with Him, as God, more than the hand of man before his face, when he is taking the closest examination of it. When we speak of places, it applies to men and angels, and not to Him as God. Space cannot confine Him, nor can He as God be eliminated from space, because He fills all, and is more than all.

Heaven and earth were not created so that He might have a

place to dwell, but were created for men and angels. Yet it pleased Him to dwell with men and angels in the homes He created for them. His filling Heaven and earth is not for His own benefit, but for the creatures He has placed in them. He existed without any Heaven and earth, and can continue to do so. A careful study of the Bible, and direction of the Holy Spirit give the information to men of earth.

### 19TH WEEK

### HIS EXISTENCE AS GOD (Cont.)

As God, He wrestled in human form with Jacob. **And Jacob was left alone; and there wrestled a man with him until the break of the day. And when he saw he prevailed not against him, he touched the hollow of his thigh; and the hollow of Jacob's thigh was out of joint, as he wrestled with him. And he said, let me go, for the day breaketh. And he said, I will not let thee go, except thou bless me. And he said unto him, What is thy name? And he said, Jacob. And he said, Thy name shall be called no more Jacob, but Israel: for as a prince hast thou power with God and with men, and hast prevailed. And Jacob asked him, and said, Tell me, I pray thee, thy name. And he said, Wherefore is it that thou dost ask after my name? And he blessed him there. And Jacob called the name of the place Peniel: for I have seen God face, to face and my life is preserved** (Genesis 32:24-30).

Although in human form He was known to Jacob as God. Regardless of His form, He impresses the human heart, when He contacts man, in such a way that he knows His Lord.

Men who deal with Him will be preserved forever in soul while living, and in soul and body after the resurrection.

### 20TH WEEK

### HIS EXISTENCE AS GOD (Cont.)

As God, He bestowed on Israel loving kindness and His great goodness before He was incarnated in human flesh. I will mention the loving kindnesses of the Lord, and the praises of

# THE LIFE OF CHRIST

the Lord, according to all that the Lord hath bestowed on us, and the great goodness toward the house of Israel, which He hath bestowed on them according to his mercies, and according to the multitude of his lovingkindnesses (Isaiah 63:7).

All of these blessings came from Christ Jesus as God. Israel knew that He was the source from which they got all their blessings, before the incarnation of Christ Jesus.

As God, He had never left His people ignorant of Himself, nor what they must do. Unlike men, He will do all that He must do for one, even though that one may rebel against Him. Israel was contrary many times, yet His loving kindness and great goodness came out from Him to them as a mighty stream, flowing from a full fountain, so much so that they acknowledged their transgressions and His loving kindness and tender mercies to them.

## 21ST WEEK

## HIS EXISTENCE AS GOD (Cont.)

As God, He saved the Israelites from their sins and from the enemies that were about them.

For He said, Surely, they are my people, children that will not lie: so he was their Saviour (Isaiah 63:8).

This brings us to the proper thinking about Our Lord. He as God was the Saviour of His chosen. He made choice of them as His to save, and Our Father accepted all that He did before the foundation of the world (Matthew 25:34; Ephesians 1:4).

Many thought, and do think now, that He became Saviour only after His birth in human flesh, but as God, He has always been Saviour of the world of men. He, the unlimited God of the universe, tells us through His prophet that Israel was His people and He was their Saviour. Inasmuch as He was their Saviour, this salvation came to them while they lived on this earth; and they existed before He came in human flesh.

## 22ND WEEK

## HIS EXISTENCE AS GOD (Cont.)

**In all their affliction he was afflicted, and the angel of his presence saved them: in his love and in his pity he redeemed them; and he bare them, and carried them all the days of old** (Isaiah 63:9).

As God, He took upon Himself all the afflictions of Israel, and saved them. He redeemed them, bore them, and carried them all the days of old. Israel found all they needed in Him for both soul and body. As God, He protected them, lifted them out of their awful condition, and carried them as a mother would her infant babe. Every time they looked unto Him, He was ready, with open hands, to rescue, and carry them to safety. With a heart full of love as a great foundation, He abundantly supplied them. Neither time nor condition did affect Him; but as God He stayed with them, and became their all sufficient Leader, Guide, Supporter and Sympathizer. Hence, He did not leave it to others, but as God He took all to Himself.

## 23RD WEEK

## HIS EXISTENCE AS GOD (Cont.)

**Then he remembered the days of old, Moses and His people, saying, Where is he that brought them up out of the sea with the shepherd of his flock? where is he that put his holy Spirit within him? That by the right hand of Moses? With his glorious arm, dividing the water before them, to make himself an everlasting name? That led them through the deep, as an horse in the wilderness, that they should not stumble?** (Isaiah 63:11-13).
They realized that, as God without a human body, He was the One that brought the Israelites through the Red Sea, making a path through the waters so that they walked on dry land. They knew that it was Christ Jesus as God, because no one could

# THE LIFE OF CHRIST

remove waters such as the Red Sea, who was not clothed in the power and might of the Deity. The prophetic inquiry was, where is He? This inquiry gives us to know that they desired Him, who was the God of the Universe, that did these things for Moses and the Israelites. The name He made in dealing with the Israelites is an everlasting one.

## 24TH WEEK

### HIS EXISTENCE AS GOD (Cont.)

**As God, He talked to the Israelites at Bochim in angelic form. And the Angel of Jehovah came up from Gilgal to Bochim. And He said, I made you to go up out of Egypt, and have brought you unto the land which I swear unto your fathers; and I said, I will never break my covenant with you; and ye shall make no league with the inhabitants of this land; ye shall throw down their altars: but ye have not obeyed my voice: why have ye done this? Wherefore I also said, I will not drive them out from before you; but they shall be as thorns in your sides, and their gods shall be as a snare unto you. And it came to pass, when the angel of the Lord spake these words unto all the children of Israel, that the people lifted up their voice, and wept** (Judges 2:2-4).

This is not a message sent by a messenger, but it is one delivered with authority, by the author of the message Himself. He who sent the Israelites out of Egypt now talks to them, because they failed to live up to the covenant they agreed upon. They wept because of the impression He made on them who had changed. He is God.

## 25TH WEEK

### HIS EXISTENCE AS GOD (Cont.)

As God, He talked to Gideon at Ophra, in Angelic form. **And the Angel of Jehovah came and sat under the oak which was** in Ophra that pertained unto Joash, the Abiezrite: and his son Gideon was beating out wheat in the wine press to hide it from the Midianites. And the Angel of Jehovah appeared unto him, and said unto him, Jehovah is with thee, thou mighty man of valor. And Gideon said unto Him, Oh, My Lord, if Jehovah is with us, why then is all this befallen us? And where are all His wondrous works which our father told us of, saying, Did not Jehovah bring us up from Egypt? But now Jehovah hath cast us off, and delivered us into the hands of Midian. And Jehovah looked upon him, and said Go in this thy might and save Israel from the hand of Midian: have not I sent thee? And he said unto Him, O my Lord, wherewith shall I save Israel? Behold, my family is the poorest in Manasseh, and I am least in my father's house. And Jehovah said unto him, surely I will be with thee and thou shalt smite the Midianites as one man (Judges 6:11-16). The other verses of this chapter and chapter seven show that He, as God, not only talked with Gideon, but did as He promised; showing His authority as God clothed in angelic form, before He came in the natural flesh of man.

## 26TH WEEK

### HIS EXISTENCE AS GOD (Cont.)

As God, He talked to Manoah and his wife, about Samson before he was conceived in the womb of his mother. He appeared to them in angelic form.

**And the angel of the Lord appeared unto the woman, and said unto her, Behold now, thou art barren, and bearest not: but thou shalt conceive, and bear a son** (Judges 13:3). **And God hearkened to the voice of Manoah; and the angel of God came again unto the woman as she sat in the field: but Manoah her husband was not with her,** (Judges 13:9). **And the angel of the Lord said unto Manoah, Of all that I said unto the woman let her beware** (Judges 13:13). **And Manoah said unto the angel of the Lord, What is thy name, that when thy sayings come to pass we may do thee honour? And the angel of the Lord said unto him, why**

# THE LIFE OF CHRIST 27

asketh thou thus after my name, seeing it is secret (Judges 13:18).

These scriptures give positive proof that Christ Jesus was "The Angel of the Lord" who appeared in angelic form to Manoah. He was Christ Jesus before He became man, the same in the spirit of God as a person, because He is truly God.

## 27TH WEEK

### THE TURNING POINT IN HIS LIFE

The change in the life of the Son as God in Spirit to Christ Jesus as the God-man, is the greatest and most mysterious miracle known to man. The how it was done is known to the Deity only. Angels do not know. Although unknown to man it nevertheless is true, true in every sense of the word. This sublime change of His form God in Spirit to the God-man, was not for Himself as such, but for the salvation of man whom He created. The Creator brought Himself into the likeness of the creature.

**Have this in mind in you which was also in Christ Jesus: who existing in the form of God, counted not the being on an equality with God a thing to be grasped, but humbled Himself, taking the form of a servant, being made in the likeness of men; and being found in fashion as a man. He humbled Himself, becoming obedient even unto death, yea, the death of the cross (Philippians 2:6-8).**

The above scripture tells the humility and self-sacrifice of the Son of God. These are set forth in His change from God to the God-man and His ignominious death on the cross. Any layman who will earnestly and prayerfully consider the above will gladly turn himself over completely into the hands of Christ Jesus, in His Spirit, to be used as long as he lives. The proper consideration of His humility and self-sacrifice will inspire laymen to take their places in the church gladly.

## 28TH WEEK

## THE TURNING POINT IN HIS LIFE (Cont.)

Why He counted not the existence as God a thing to be grasped or held on to (Philemon 2:6, 7) was because holding on to His existence as God would have left man outside of the kingdom eternally. His great heart filled with the fountain of love, moved Him to empty Himself of all glory as God and humiliate Himself that man could be exalted again in his first creation. The thorough knowledge of this will move all laymen, who have His love, to take first place in His church, and feel highly honored after doing so.

Inasmuch as He gave up all of His happiness, joy and pleasure as God for man; laymen should be proud to give up all for Him.

To remain as God as such was the best for Him, but it was a curse to man. He made the humility, and sacrifice voluntarily. In turn, every layman should not wait for someone to appoint him a place in the church, but voluntarily take the place prepared for him by Christ Jesus. When he does so, there will come renewed power in the Church of Christ Jesus from the Holy Spirit's manifestation day by day, the necessary things for our day (Matthew 20:28; 2 Corinthians 6:1-10; 8:9).

## 29TH WEEK

## CHRIST JESUS, THE GOD-MAN

**And The Word was made flesh, and dwelt among us, (and we beheld His glory, the glory as of the only begotten of the Father,) full of grace and truth** (John 1:14).

We have here stated the change made in the life of Christ Jesus as God, to Christ Jesus the God-man. The statement is just as true as God Himself is true. "The Word became flesh" is saying God became man. Word is God, and flesh is man. Hence we have

## THE LIFE OF CHRIST

in His Personality the God-man, two natures—human and Divine.

The God-man, who is Christ Jesus, dwelt among us to save us and to show us how to let Him save others through us. Man's salvation and safety, all depended on the attitude of the Deity toward us, all of which had to be displayed in the God-man. All heaven depended on Him, and all earth depended on Him. He became the burden-bearer for all. The Deity centers in Him. Men center all in Him. Angels center all in Him. In fact His becoming flesh carried out the exact idea of Our Father for man's salvation (Matthew 1:21; Acts 4:12; 10:43; 1 Timothy 2:5, 6).

### 30TH WEEK

### CHRIST JESUS, THE GOD-MAN (Cont.)

**"Dwelt among us," "Immanuel." Therefore the Lord himself shall give you a sign; Behold, a virgin shall conceive, and bear a son, and shall call his name Immanuel** (Isaiah 7:14).

This prophecy, given by Our Father in His Spirit through Isaiah, was fulfilled when Christ Jesus was born (Matthew 1:18-25).

It was absolutely necessary for God to dwell with men after man permitted the devil to come into his world. It was not the will of our Father for the devil to have charge of anything in man's world because of his deception. But He permitted it to be so, because it was man's pleasure to disobey Him, and obey the devil.

The first thing the devil did, after given privilege in man's world, was to get his hands on the greatest glory our Father had here, which was man. Inasmuch as that was done it was necessary that God must dwell on the earth in human form, that He might restore all that had been destroyed by the devil. Hence we have **"He dwelt among us." "Immanuel."** The only hope of man is "Immanuel." Man permitted the destructive being to come in, doubting Our Father's word, and the devil was more than he could handle. Thus God had to come to his rescue by dwelling with us in Christ Jesus. How wonderful.

## 31ST WEEK

## CHRIST JESUS, THE GOD-MAN (Cont.)

"**Dwelt among us.**" "Emmanuel." The only hope of one who has been over-powered by one who is stronger than he, is that a stronger one than he come to his rescue . . . How can one enter the house of the strong man, and spoil his goods, except he first bind the strong man? And then he will spoil his house, (Matthew 12:29).

The devil entered the home of man and bound him, and spoiled his goods, and Christ Jesus entered the stolen home of the devil, and bound him, and spoiled his goods thus restoring man's home to him, and leaving the devil bound for all who will believe in Christ Jesus.

It is a thought that makes all happy, who believe in the presence of Christ Jesus, in His Spirit, dwelling on the earth among us. His presence is destructive to all that the devil has done, can do or will do. His Presence in the world where sin is, has made the heaven for all who will believe it. No heart, no home, no school, no church, no community, no town, no city, no state, no country, no family, no race, no nation, and no world should exist unless Christ Jesus in His spirit dwells in it.

## 32ND WEEK

## CHRIST JESUS, THE GOD-MAN (Cont.)

"**We beheld His glory, the glory as of the only begotten of the Father.**" Here we have expressed in words, and seen in Christ Jesus the God-man, the very image of Our Father. The Father is the glory of the Son, and the Son is the glory of the Father. The Son is seen always in the Father, and the Father is seen always in the Son. **If ye had known me, ye should have known my Father**

# THE LIFE OF CHRIST

also: and from henceforth ye know him, and have seen him. Have I been so long time with you, and yet hast thou not known me, Philip? he that hath seen me hath seen the Father; and how sayest thou then, Shew us the Father? Believest thou not that I am in the Father, and the Father in me? the words that I speak unto you I speak not of myself: but the Father that dwelleth in me He doeth the works. Believe me that I am in the Father, and the Father in me: or else believe me for the very works' sake (John 14:7-11).

All the splendor of Our Father for man was put out in the world through Christ Jesus. The human eye never looked upon such glory before, as was seen in the beautiful life of the God-man.

## 33RD WEEK

### CHRIST JESUS, THE GOD-MAN (Cont.)

'**We beheld His glory.**" Divinity wrapped in humanity is the most glorious scene that the human eye ever beheld on earth. Divinity cannot be hidden by humanity. Humanity is delighted to let Divinity shine out through it; hence it always gives itself over into the hands of Divinity. "That saves humanity, and humanity wants all to know when Divinity comes into it that Divinity is present.

To see a man taken completely into the Divine mind and the very image of God, is one of the greatest miracles, and one of the most glorious sights seen by men or angels on this earth of ours. "**We beheld His glory**" thrills the souls of men through and through, who have been made again by recreation or regeneration (Luke 9:32; John 2:11; 17:22, 24; 2 Peter 1:16; 1 John 1:1).

Christ Jesus, in the glory of His Father manifested, never passed by any one or walked the road, street or ever moved out among men but that all eyes had to look upon Him in astonished amazement.

## 34TH WEEK

"**We beheld His glory.**" One of the greatest expressions coming out of the mouth of humanity is this one. **We beheld His glory.** Moses said: **Show me, I pray Thee, thy Glory,** (Exodus 33:18), John says, **We beheld His glory** (John 1:14). The Holy Spirit put it into the mind of Moses, and his soul longed to see Divinity clothed in humanity. Because of His faithfulness to our Father, and it being the delight of Our Father to give the faithful the desires of their hearts, He had Moses to stand at an appointed place and gave him an opportunity to see Christ Jesus in this glory that John spoke about long before He came to earth.

Upon the mountain of transfiguration, when Christ Jesus was seen in all of His glory as never before by the apostles, they did not want to come down because of the glory scene.

Any layman, who by faith will look up and see Christ Jesus in His glory, will take his place in the church, the lay mountain of transfiguration and remain until his departure from this earth.

## 35TH WEEK

### CHRIST JESUS, THE GOD-MAN (Cont.)

"**Full of grace and truth.**" The fountain of all grace and Truth is Christ Jesus. This Grace and Truth (Christ Jesus) is all for humanity. Being full of it, no one could prevent Him from giving it in abundance unto man. Grace and truth are not a part of God Our Father, but is God our Father.

When Christ Jesus in His Spirit through Peter says, **But grow in grace and knowledge of our Lord and Saviour Jesus Christ,** (2 Peter 3:18), He means grow in the Spirit of Christ Jesus, who gives to all who ask wisdom and knowledge. Christ Jesus Himself said in John 8:32, **You shall know the Truth and the Truth shall make you free.**

And in John 14:6, He says **I am the way, the truth and the life.**

Christ Jesus was full of His Father to the end that whoever saw Him saw the Father. Whoever received Him received the Father and the Holy Spirit.

# THE LIFE OF CHRIST

Being the Godman, He brought to earth a full supply of Heaven, that man might have a plenty of God in him, that all of the devil might be entirely destroyed in him.

## 36TH WEEK

### CHRIST JESUS, THE GOD-MAN (Cont.)

**Through What He became, The God-Man**

The Holy Spirit, who is God also, overshadowed Mary the virgin, and she conceived and gave birth to a Son, and called His name Jesus, who should save His people from their sins (Matthew 1:18, 21).

The long-looked for "Seed of the woman" has come to earth.

Through the woman He got His human nature, and from the Holy Spirit He got His Divine nature. As God, the Deity is seen in all His deeds and actions. As man, humanity is displayed in all His human endeavors to the end that He was known to those who lived about Him as "The Man of Galilee."

Being both, He became the One who united in "One Person," the two natures through which Our Father got all that He required to reconcile Himself, and man got all that was necessary for his salvation.

## 37TH WEEK

### CHRIST JESUS, THE GOD-MAN (Cont.)

**As A Child**

As a child, He grew and waxed strong, filled with wisdom: **And the grace of God was upon Him** (Luke 2:40). The text above shows the human side of Christ Jesus. **He grew.** It is the nature of humanity to grow. We do not conceive nor is it revealed to us that God as such grows. Divinity is the source from whence came humanity, and every thing else gets its growth; but Divinity never grows, because Divinity is perfect, not only in kind, but in degree as well. Not in the human sense of perfection but in the Divine sense and in all that is God.

**Waxed strong.** This cannot be said of Him as God, because He as God is the embodiment of strength. Hence this truly is said of Him as man. "Filled with Wisdom" is the human side, because as God He is not only filled with wisdom, but is Wisdom. "The Grace of God was upon Him." This is human because as God He is all grace. We have here truly the human side.

## 38TH WEEK

### CHRIST JESUS, THE GOD-MAN (Cont.)

Starting with Him as a child brings us truly to His Human side, because God is never spoken of as a child. Divine Beings are never thought of as children, but this is applied always to humanity. Hence we are dealing with Him strictly from His human side. As such we are required to come up to all He requires of us as such.

He has never and never will require of us to do as He, or to be like Him as God. All commands given to us to be like Him are not from the standpoint of Himself as God, but as The Man Christ Jesus. Inasmuch as He grew, waxed strong, and was filled with wisdom and the grace of God was upon Him, He also requires of us to grow, wax strong, be filled with wisdom and the grace of God to be upon us from the time we are spiritually born and throughout our Christian careers.

When such is done by us as Christians, we come into full growth as His children, and become worth our full value in the kingdom.

## 39TH WEEK

### CHRIST JESUS, THE GOD-MAN (Cont.)

For humanity to be perfect, it must be filled with Divinity. Divinity

# THE LIFE OF CHRIST

gives perfection to humanity. He requires of us to be all that He commands. He commands us to be all that He will make us. And He will make us all that Our Father requires if we will let Him (John 15:5; Philemon 4:13).

When the human soul possesses the life of Our Father, it has "The Eternal Life" within. When Eternal Life is within, Christ is there. When Christ Jesus is there we have more power on the in side to keep us than there is on the outside to destroy us. He that is within you (Christ Jesus) is greater than he (the devil) that is in the world (1 John 4:5). The Almighty power is in us when we have been regenerated. While we know the mighty power (devil) is in the world, but Almighty Power (God) is the greatest, and we need not fear what the mighty in the world may attempt to do. Divine Power always conquers in the end. Regardless to what the beginning may seem to be, when Divinity is within, the end will always be grand and glorious.

## 40TH WEEK

## CHRIST JESUS, THE GOD-MAN (Cont.)

Since He has become fully man, there is no excuse for us to not be all He requires of us. He has gone before in human flesh and fixed everything for us. Also He has returned in Spirit, and dwells with us to help us to come up to the requirements of Our Father. Read John 14:1-17.

From His birth He set the example for every layman. No birth was as His. No life was as His. No death was as His. Laymen ought to run if necessary to take the lead in His church. To be a leader for Him should be the greatest ambition of every man.

His existence as God and His birth as man laid a foundation for Heaven and earth to build any superstructure our Father wants to construct. All men should make Christ Jesus their standard in all their dealings with men, in all walks of life; thereby, bringing the world in which we live into perfect union with Our Father through Christ Jesus.

## 41ST WEEK

### CHRIST JESUS, THE GOD-MAN (Cont.)

Why did He come in human flesh? To carry out the will of Our Father . . . **Sacrifice and offering thou wouldest not, but a body hast thou prepared me; . . . I am come to do thy will, O God** (Hebrews 10:5, 6). Our Father's will is to save the world of men. **Look unto me, and be ye saved, all the ends of the earth: for I am God, and there is none else** (Isaiah 45:22).

Without being clothed in human flesh, Christ Jesus as God would not have taken our place as sinners. Accepting human flesh put Him in the exact world where man lived. It also made Him our nearest kin. It put Him where He could say to us do as I did. It fills the purpose of Our Father.

Adam let us down while in the body, and Christ Jesus had to pick us up while in the human body. Had He gotten out of the human body before He died spiritually, He could not have saved us. It was in this prepared body, where the eternal sacrifice was made that satisfied our Father, and fixed it so that all could escape hell, who believed in Him as Saviour of the world.

## 42ND WEEK

### CHRIST JESUS, THE GOD-MAN (Cont.)

What He did as a child. His first actions are found in Luke 2:41-47. At the age of twelve He was found in the Temple among the Rabbis, both listening to them and asking them questions. All who heard Him were amazed at His questions, answers and understanding. When asked by His mother why He remained, He said, ''Did you not realize that I had to be in my Father's house. (Business in the authorized version should have been translated house). We see here He knew from the beginning what He came in human flesh to do.

Laymen should be taught early that their purpose in the world

# THE LIFE OF CHRIST

is to do the will of Our Father. Not knowing it from natural childhood it should be taught from the cradle of regeneration by the minister of Our Father. It is easy to continue right when starting early.

His parents did not understand the words He spoke. From a child He knew the time He was to be in His Father's house. Many laymen have been in the church for years, and do not know yet the time to be at the house of worship. The laymen who do know and are found there at all times, are blessed far beyond those who do not know. Christ Jesus made His Father's will His biggest business. All laymen must enter into the same spirit as the Christ. Don't be satisfied at home on the Lord's day, nor any time when needed at the meeting house.

## 43RD WEEK

### CHRIST JESUS, THE GOD-MAN (Cont.)

What He did as a child, (Luke 2:51). He went home with His parents after leaving the Temple, to Nazareth, and was always obedient to them. The Bible history brings Him before us no more until He is about 30 years old, being subject to His parents naturally all these years, but to His Father spiritually. No man was His Teacher. He was wiser than all the men of His day. He spent these 18 years in the school of Our Father, who was His only Teacher. All of His wisdom and knowledge was used for Him from whom He received it.

Laymen ought to learn of Him, and then use all the wisdom and knowledge gotten in His service. He will give to anyone wisdom and knowledge for all that one is to do, if he will ask for it.

If any one is lacking in wisdom, let him ask it from the God who gives to all men freely and without upbraiding; and it will be given to him (James 1:5).

Inasmuch as it is necessary to know, be, and do, all laymen should spend more time with Him in Spirit thoroughly preparing for the work of our Father. Do it while the day of our time still is upon us, that when night comes we can lie down in sweet repose.

## 44TH WEEK

### CHRIST JESUS, THE GOD-MAN (Cont.)

#### His Crowning Point Of Preparation

It was at that time that Jesus came from Nazareth of Galilee, and was baptized by John in the Jordan; and as soon as He rose from the water He saw the sky cleft asunder, and the Spirit like a dove descending upon Him, and a voice from the sky saying: **Thou art my Son. My beloved; in Thee is my delight** (Mark 1.9-11).

To know when to do anything and what to do, is to follow strictly the example of Christ Jesus. The time to leave Nazareth for the Jordan to be baptized, was kept in His mind and not one moment passed. Laymen should be careful to see that what they are to do should be done on time all the time.

The Spirit and the voice of the Father speaking gave Him great joy, inspiration and courage to go forward in His work. Always, when one does the will of our Father, He always makes it known that He is pleased with him, by some kind of a sign. The voice and the Spirit were true signs that Jesus was the Messiah. One, a sign seen, and the other a voice heard.

After guaranteeing His completion of His work by His baptism, He was anointed by the Holy Spirit for what He came to do. No layman can fit into the work of the Master without baptism and the leadership of the Holy Spirit (Matthew 3:16; Mark 1:10).

## 45TH WEEK

### CHRIST JESUS, THE GOD-MAN (Cont.)

#### His Crowning Point Of Preparation. (Cont.)

Then the spirit drove him at once into the desert, and He remained in the desert 40 days, tempted by Satan; and he was

# THE LIFE OF CHRIST

among the wild beasts, and angels ministered unto Him (Mark 1:12, 13).

Thorough preparation is not made without the acid test. This temptation forty days and nights was an acid test in the life of Christ Jesus. When one goes through the acid test without faltering or failing, one need not doubt his ability to accomplish his task.

He was thoroughly tested by Satan so much so, that the devil did not have anything else to present to Him when Christ drove him away. Exhausting the devil of all he had, brought Him to the end of His thorough preparation.

Angels ministered unto Him at the end of the temptation, proving to the world of men that Our Father will supply all our needs, and at the right time, if we will only stand the tests that come to us. He was in the wilderness among the wild beasts, but conquered just the same. If it is in a layman to overcome evil, put there by the Holy Spirit, he will do so, regardless of where he is or who he is with.

## 46TH WEEK

### CHRIST JESUS, THE GOD-MAN (Cont.)

The time He began His ministry, and Jesus Himself when He began to teach, was about thirty years of age (Luke 3:23). After His thorough preparation under His Father He then began His mission; He truly set the proper example for all men, (first—in His birth, humbly born; second—in His childhood, knowing and doing; third—in His youth and young manhood—thoroughly preparing; Fourth—in His manhood—doing all that He came into human flesh to do.

All laymen, who follow His lead, will accomplish all that they came in the world to do both spiritually and physically. At this tender age (30) He stretches out full length in service, until it all ended on the Cross of Calvary.

When laymen rightly see all this by faith and will feel the impression made by the Holy Spirit, who is now in the earth to impress upon the hearts and lives of all, who know Him theoretical ly and experientially, they will gladly labor in the field of His kingdom without reserve. May all hasten to that point, and fill every church with faithful service.

## 47TH WEEK

### CHRIST JESUS, THE GOD-MAN (Cont.)

He came into the world to supply human needs for body and soul: (A) For body, Healing it of its diseases (1) Giving sight to the blind, (Matthew 9:27:31; Mark 8:22-26; John 9:1-7). Sin deprived man of his natural sight, and no one could restore that sight, but our Father in His Son through His Spirit. No human skill on earth can produce an eye or heal one that is diseased. Christ Jesus, the great **Physician, was and is** the only man that could do so. He will heal through physicians today when need be, if they will only have faith in Him, for without faith in Him there can be no healing of eyes.

## 48TH WEEK

### CHRIST JESUS, THE GOD-MAN (Cont.)

(2) Opening the deaf ears (Matthew 11:5; Mark 7:32, 37; Luke 7:12). The sense of hearing is so valuable to man, to deprive him of it is to rob him of joy and happiness that can come to him from no other source.

Men who were deaf needed their ears opened, but sin had so affected human ability to do so, that the Christ was and is the only one that could meet this need.

(3) Make the dumb to speak (Matthew 9:32, 33; 12:22; 15:30, 31; Mark 7:33-37).

Our Father gave man the blessed gift to speak, so that the thoughts of one mind could be conveyed to another, and thereby make men happy. Dumbness is the work of the devil to prevent

# THE LIFE OF CHRIST 41

man from enjoying the blessings our Father gave him. Jesus restored man to this happiness again by removing his dumbness.

## 49TH WEEK

### CHRIST JESUS, THE GOD-MAN (Cont.)

(4) Made the lame walk (Matthew 11:5; 15:31; 21:14; Luke 7:22). To walk is to be able to put into execution the thoughts of the mind. When one is deprived of the ability to walk, he is greatly hindered. Jesus is the only one who can give back to man his soundness so that he can walk.

(5) Healed all the diseases of the body (Matthew 4:23; 9:35; 10:1; Mark 1:34; Luke 4:40; 6:17; John 5:4). Christ Jesus was, is and shall ever be the only man that could, can, and will heal the diseases of man. He knows how, when, and what to do in every case.

## 50TH WEEK

### CHRIST JESUS, THE GOD-MAN (Cont.)

(6) He fed all who were hungry, that came to Him (Matthew 14:15; 15:28; Mark 7:24; 6:30; Luke 9:10; John 6:1-14).

He is the only man that can create food, and feed starving humanity. He is the only man that is feeding the world today. All human supplies of food and raiment come from Him.

(7) He raised the bodies from the dead (Luke 8:11-18; 8:49-55; John 11:38-44). Every person that has ever been raised and will be raised from the dead was and will be by the power of the Man, Christ Jesus.

We see from the above, that He met every need of the body, and today will continue to do so, if men will only have faith in Him. Let every layman give Him credit for the supply of human needs, and teach others to do so. He is more than worthy of such. All laymen should present their bodies as living sacrifices unto our Father for what He has done for them through Christ (Romans

12:1).

## 51ST WEEK

### CHRIST JESUS, THE GOD-MAN (Cont.)

(B) For Soul. (a) Redeeming it from the prison of sin, (Psalm 130:7; Matthew 20:28; Romans 3:24; 1 Corinthians 1:30; Colossians 1:14; Titus 2:14). The greatest darkness man was ever placed in was when he was shut up in the prison of sin. He lost his sonship, and became a child of the evil one. No one could go into the prison and deliver him but the one man, Christ Jesus, which He did happily. He paid the price (Acts 20:28; 1 Corinthians 6:20; 1 Peter 1:18; Revelation 5:9). He will deliver every soul who will believe.

Every layman should give himself in active service to Our Father, for the redemptive price Christ paid for him. No man could do so, and no man did do so but Christ; hence the soul of every layman should be presented to Our Father for Him to dwell in forever.

## 52ND WEEK

### CHRIST JESUS, THE GOD-MAN (Cont.)

(b) Supply it with all its needs. (1) Regeneration (John 3:5; Ephesians 5:26; Titus 3:5).

(2) Sanctification (Acts 20:32; 26:18; Romans 6:22; Hebrews 12:14).

(3) The Holy Spirit who supplies it with everything needful (John 14:16, 17).

When one is filled with the Spirit of Our Father, He being God and Creator of all things, that one is fully prepared to have body and soul provided for.

The Man, who provides for the complete needs of the whole man, should be honored, adored, worshipped, and given all he requires of men at all times and in every place. This Man is Christ-Jesus, the world's only Saviour and Lord.

Let every layman exalt Him, and rededicate his life to Him.

**ONE YEAR'S STUDY**

**ON**

**MAN**

**FOR THE BROTHERHOOD**

## PURPOSE

The study of man for one year from a Biblical standpoint, is for the purpose of having the layman see who he is, that a consciousness might be awakened in him, so that he may take his place in the church of our Father, and lead in the church as he wants to in the world.

The layman is the one to so imbibe the Spirit of Christ Jesus, so as to have His Kingdom come on earth that a new world may dawn upon humanity. It cannot be done until every layman takes his place in the church. The man-power must be reharnessed for Our Father, and the ministry does not mean to rest until every layman has given to Our Father his soul, body and spirit with all that it may possess. The world must be changed, and this change must be brought on by the unity of laymen and ministers, uniting in the Spirit of Christ, and pushing the battle to the gate of righteousness.

# ONE YEAR'S COURSE—MEN'S UNION

## LESSONS

### 1ST WEEK

### THE ORIGIN OF MAN

(a) He was created in the image and likeness of His Creator (God), the first part of Genesis 1:27. (b) His body was formed out of the dust of the ground, the first part of Genesis 2:7, 3:23. The ground was created, hence he was created (Genesis 1:27). We see in these scriptures that he is the direct creation of God. He was created a full grown man and not evolved from some other species. He is the first human seed spoken of in creation. From this seed came all human beings that earth has (Acts 17:26).

### 2ND WEEK

### HE WAS WONDERFULLY CREATED AND MADE

**Thine hands have made me and fashioned me together round about; yet thou dost destroy me. Remember, I beseech thee, that thou hast made me as the clay; and wilt thou bring me into dust again? Hast thou not poured me out as milk, and curdled me like cheese? Thou hast clothed me with skin and flesh, and hast fenced me with bones and sinews** (Job 10:8-11). Being wonderfully created and made like God, there is not anything nor anybody that can keep him from being like God, but himself lined up with Satan.

### 3RD WEEK

### HE WAS WONDERFULLY CREATED AND MADE (Cont.)

**I will praise thee; for I am fearfully and wonderfully made: marvellous are thy works; and that my soul knoweth right**

well . . . **My substance was not hid from thee, when I was made in secret, and curiously wrought in the lowest parts of the earth. Thine eyes did see my substance, yet being unperfect; and in thy book all my members were written, which in continuance were fashioned, when as yet there was none of them** (Psalm 139:14-16). Knowing how wonderfully he is made will help to bring him into his own. No other creature is made just as he.

## 4TH WEEK

### HE WAS WONDERFULLY CREATED AND MADE (Cont.)

**As thou knowest not what is the way of the spirit, nor how the bones do grow in the womb of her that is with child: even so thou knowest not the works of God who maketh all** (Ecclesiastes 11:5). It is unthinkable for one to read how wonderfully man is created and made, and still believe he came from some lower species than himself. His form and creation are above all he sees around him. He is created and made to master all about him in the time world. He should use his wondrous nature in producing wonderful things for humanity and God.

## 5TH WEEK

### HE WAS CREATED IN THE IMAGE OF THE DEITY

The image consists of the following, (a) spirituality. God is a Spirit, and His worshippers must worship Him in spirit and in truth (John 4:24). Let the Lord, the God of the spirits of all flesh, set a man over the congregation (Numbers 27:16). Shall we not be in subjection to the Father of spirits and live)? Inasmuch as God is Spirit, so must one be who is created in His image. God is spirit and invisible, so is the real spirit man. God cannot be seen with the natural eye, nor can the real man on the inside of the body be seen naturally.

## 6TH WEEK

### (a) SPIRITUALLY

God breathed in man the breath of life, and man became a living soul (Genesis 2:7). The burden of the word of the Lord for Israel, saith the Lord, which stretcheth forth the heavens, and layeth the foundation of the earth, and formeth the spirit of man within him. The real man is on the inside of the outside man. The one on the inside does the thinking, the willing, the choosing and the executing of all deeds and actions through the outside man. The outside man is the body taken from the ground. The inside man is the spirit created by the Father of spirits.

## 7TH WEEK

### SPIRITUALLY (Cont.)

The spirit of man is the candle of the Lord, searching all the inward parts of the belly (Proverbs 20:27). Then shall the dust return to the earth as it was: and the spirit shall return unto God who gave it (Ecclesiastes 12:7). The spirit of man is not a part of God's Spirit, but is the spirit-man that God created. God put him in a house of flesh to rule over it, and bring it in complete control under his spirit. Spirit rules matter and matter does not rule spirit.

## 8TH WEEK

### (b) IMMORTALITY

Now unto the King Eternal, immortal, invisible, the only God, be honor and glory forever and ever (1 Timothy 1:17). **Whoso sheddeth man's blood, by man shall his blood be shed: for in the image of God made he man** (Genesis 9:6). Inasmuch as God is immortal and man is made in His image, he is also immortal. Spirit is indestructible. Man had a beginning but will have no end, like the one who created him. He will live forever regardless of what he is, sinner or Christian, no end to the joy of the saved, and no end to the sorrow of the lost.

## 9TH WEEK

## (c) INTUTITIVE KNOWLEDGE AND REASONING

And out of the ground—the Lord—God formed every beast of the field, and every fowl of the air; and brought them unto Adam to see what he would call them: and whatsoever Adam called every living creature, that was the name thereof. And Adam gave names to all cattle, and to the fowl of the air; and to every beast of the field (Genesis 2:19, 20). . . . Put on the new man, that is being renewed unto knowledge after the image of Him (Colossians 3:10). No one could give names to a nameless host, such as the above, unless possessing the knowledge and reasoning power of God. Knowledge is one of the main qualities of God's image. To take charge of all God has brought forth into the world and master them as He requires, there must be the greatest reasoning and knowledge used.

## 10TH WEEK

## (d) DIGNITY OF PRESENCE

And the fear of you and the dread of you shall be upon every beast of the earth, and upon every bird of the heaven, with all wherewith the ground teameth, and all the fishes of the sea, into your hands are they delivered (Genesis 9:2).

The image of God seen in man by the other living creatures, makes them fear him. His presence on land makes even the master beast fear and tremble. His presence in the sky makes the king bird fear and fly away. His presence in the sea makes the greatest monster run and hide. All men, who live like animals, fear men who live like Jesus, who is the very image of the Father.

## 11TH WEEK

### (a) UPRIGHTNESS AND HOLINESS

**Lo, this only have I found, that God hath made man upright; but they have sought out many inventions (Ecclesiastes 7:29) . . . . Put on the new man, which after God is created in righteousness and true holiness** (Ephesians 4:24).

No one could be created in the image of the Deity, who did not possess holiness; because He is the very embodiment of holiness. The upright man shows forth the Deity, and the image of the Deity is seen in the uprightness of man. The Deity constantly and continually talking with man when created gives us to know that he was holy. All the children of God are holy.

## 12TH WEEK

### COMMANDS GIVEN HIM

**(a) Be fruitful, and multiply, and fill the earth** (Genesis 1:28). This command was given before sin entered the world. Man, as the first human seed, must put out the fruit that had been put in him by our Creator. Be fruitful means be full of fruit, human fruit. This human fruit was a blessing that he was blessed with and the blessing must be spread all over the world by him. The command to be fruitful was not a command to create, but not to hinder that which was already created by Jehovah, the very thing that many have done and are doing. The fruit must be increased not by addition, but by multiplication. This process is why the rapidity of humanity has been of such in the world. Every continent and island must be filled by human beings.

## 13TH WEEK

### BE FRUITFUL

God said to **Noah and his sons, "Be fruitful, multiply and** replenish the earth." (Genesis 9:1). **And you, be ye fruitful, and multiply; bring forth abundantly in the earth, and multiply therein** (Genesis 9:7). We studied in the twelfth week the giving of this command to Adam before sin had entered into the world. In this, the thirteenth week, we study the same command as it is given to Noah after sin had entered into the world. In the first case, it was a command to multiply and fill the earth. In the case of Noah and his sons, it was to multiply and replenish the earth. There could not be a replenishing until after the filling. The world had been destroyed by water, and therefore must be replenished by the second race-head. The multiplied fruit of humanity had to be before the whole earth could be subdued.

## 14TH WEEK

### (b) SUBDUE THE EARTH

Subdue the earth mastering the fish in the sea, the birds of the air, and every living creature that crawls on the earth (Genesis 1:28). Man was commanded to bring every creature under his management. To be able to do this the power of mastery was given him by Our Father. Before He gives command, He always gives ability to do what He commands. There is no excuse given by man that will stand or be considered by our Father, because commands come because of the power given to carry them out. No power to execute, no command given. The ability to use all animals, beasts and birds, also earth, wind, water and fire was given to man that he might subdue all under him, being directed by Jehovah.

## 15TH WEEK

### (c) HAVE DOMINION OVER ALL THINGS

Have dominion over the fish of the sea, and over the fowl of the air, and over every living thing that moveth upon the earth (Genesis 1:28). Our Father gave man dominion over things that were lower in the scale of creation than he. This first man understood it well. He has not given him dominion over men by command, because every man was created equal. Equals must not try to have dominion over equals, but must reason together over matters necessary, and co-operate in all of earth's affairs. The Man, Christ Jesus, is the only man that has been given dominion over men. Anyone else who tries it always gets into trouble, because he transcends his authority.

## 16TH WEEK

## HIS FOOD

**. . . Behold, I have given you every herb bearing seed, which is upon the face of all the earth, and every tree, in the which is the fruit of a tree yielding seed; to you it shall be for meat** (Genesis 1:29). The first man before he sinned did not kill any living thing for food. It was provided in the fruit of the herbs and trees. He did not know what it was to take life, to sustain life, until he fell from the holy state that he was placed in by Our Father. When the human family became so sinful that all had to be destroyed by the flood, then our Father gave to Noah and his sons, the second race-head, the privilege to sustain life by killing things that had life. This should keep in man's mind the awful condition brought about by sin, and as a Christian, the urge to shun the dreaded evil, through faith in Our Father.

## 17TH WEEK

## HIS FIRST HOME

**And the Lord God planted a garden eastward, in Eden; and there he put the man whom he had formed** (Genesis 2:8). Everything necessary for man's happiness was in this garden, all kinds of fruit and herbs, that would keep the body in a perfectly healthy condition, and no sin to disease the body or soul. This was a home that no one who did not live at that time could imagine. His wife was the best, produced by Divine hands, a perfect form, a beautiful face, and like Adam in body and soul as to unity, and the very one for all his comfort. They were filled with all the joy that Our Father blessed them with, which was unspeakable. She faithfully performed her duty as a help-meet. Our Father made the unity and officiated when they married.

## 18TH WEEK

### HIS FIRST HOME (Cont.)

The home was governed by Divine laws, and as long as they were obeyed, the home was happy. He was commanded not to eat the fruit from the tree in the midst of the garden of good and evil, if so he would die (Genesis 2:17). To not obey a Divine command has always resulted in death. He lived as long as he obeyed, and died when he could no longer obey. The same holds good today with men. Death did not come into this home until the head of the home disobeyed. The law was given to the man who was head. All men should be the heads of the home. No man is much of a man who does not head the home. Man should obey His Creator in the home, and his wife should obey him. Each one should take his and her place, and fill it well.

## 19TH WEEK

### WHERE MAN'S WIFE CAME FROM

Every man should seek the Lord for his wife, and every woman should seek the Lord for her husband. When He unites two, they will remain. God, the Eternal, shaped into a woman, the rib taken out of man, and brought her unto the man (Genesis 2:21, 22). They cannot be united in all efforts put forth, when they are not united in spirit. To get one so he may be united, she must be given to him by Our Father. He who makes the choice for the two will also provide the way for them to meet and unite, regardless of the distance they are born apart. Divorces will cease, when passion, good looks, money and other things cease to be the cause of the union of man and woman.

## 20TH WEEK

### WHAT A MAN MUST DO AFTER MARRIAGE

**Therefore shall a man leave his father and his mother, and shall cleave unto his wife: and they shall be one flesh** (Genesis 2:24). Man is to remain in the home of his parents until he takes to himself a wife. When this is done, he must leave and go into a home, where he is the head, and his wife is his helpmeet. It is seldom that any two heads and help-meets get along in the same house. It was not intended from the beginning that such would be, but that each man head his own family in his own house. The man cannot fully develop, nor his wife, being governed by others. As husband and wife live together and bless the world, so Christ and His Church live together, and save and bless the world.

## 21ST WEEK

### MAN'S FALL

So when the woman saw that the tree was good to eat and delightful to see, desirable to look upon, she took some of the fruit and ate it; she also gave some to her husband and he ate. Then the eyes of them both were opened, and they realized that they were naked (Genesis 3:6, 7a). It was this act of Adam and Eve that caused the spiritual death of them, and all the human family. Spiritually, he died the very day he ate and gradually the body began dying. Believing the devil's word gives death. Believing God's word gives life. The fruit eaten was the words of the devil believed. When born naturally, we are inclined to believe the devil rather than God. Disbelief unites us from God. Belief ties us back again. We fall when we disbelieve Him, and rise when we believe Him.

## 22ND WEEK

### RESULTS OF THE FALL

(a) Man became naked and ashamed. Before the fall they were

not ashamed. Both of them, the man and his wife, were naked but they felt no shame (Genesis 2:25). When sin enters one's heart, it is always accompanied by shame. Shame would be unknown to the human family had we all not sinned in Adam. Anyone who is ashamed today, it is because sin is found somewhere in that life. Before he sinned he was naked, but not ashamed. Shame is one of the diseases that has come to man because of sin. It is embarrassing to have such a thing as shame hung on to the life of one. One is prevented from full enjoyment, and robbed of a world of contentment when one is filled with shame.

## 23RD WEEK
## RESULTS OF THE FALL (Cont.)

(b) Not able to make that which is necessary to hide nakedness. Cannot even select the proper material. **So they stitched fig leaves together and made themselves girdles** (Genesis 3:7a). When man sins, he does not know even what to do when he awakes to find himself in the throes of that awful condition, which separates him from his Creator. Every step he takes from relief makes his condition worse. From one degree of ignorance to another he goes, until he is lost completely in mind, and body. His own hiding place becomes nothing to him, and yet he does not know any other.

## 24TH WEEK
## RESULTS OF THE FALL (Cont.)

(c) Tries to hide from the presence of God the Eternal. In the cool of the day when they heard the sound of God the Eternal walking in the park, the man and his wife hid from the presence of God the Eternal among the trees of the park (Genesis 3:8). Anyone that tries to hide has within him or her that element of sin that cause such. Every crime committed by man, the devil makes him feel that he can save himself from it by hiding, a greater deception than that which caused the thing committed. There is no hiding place from any sin, because it is a part of the man in his heart, and no man can hide from his own heart wherein is the writing upon the conscience, that stands before his mind, the brilliant light of the soul, and readily interpreted by the Reader within.

## 25TH WEEK

## RESULTS OF THE FALL (Cont.)

(d) Afraid, I heard the sound of you in the park, and I was afraid (Genesis 3:10). Sin always makes afraid, anyone who commits it. To be afraid is to be tormented. Because fear has torment in it so deeply, that it can be removed only when the fear itself is removed. It is one of the things that keeps men from thinking and acting normally. When men fear because of sin it always makes one a coward. Slavish fear hinders one from reaching the proper conclusion as to what to do, after having fallen into sin by disobedience. Fear, as brought on by not living up to the commands of our Father, binds one to an evil that continues to lead one into the deeper ideas of destruction, and that prevents one from presenting himself to the One that will save from sin and destruction.

## 26TH WEEK

## RESULTS OF THE FALL (Cont.)

(e) Putting the sin on another. The man said, "The woman you gave me as a companion, she gave me some fruit from the tree, and I ate it." The woman said, "I ate because the serpent beguiled me" (Genesis 3:12, 13). This curse came down through the human family. Men are today saying I did it because this caused it, and that caused it. Men should face their own sins like they ought. Instead of trying to shift the responsibility one should confess his or her sins and ask for forgiveness. Repentance and confession will put one in the right attitude before His Maker, better than all the excuses he may try to find (1 John 1:9). Each must account for his own sins, hence one blaming another will not alter the case at all.

## 27TH WEEK

### RESULTS OF THE FALL (Cont.)

(f) Pain. To the woman, He said, "I will make child-birth a sore pain for you; you shall have pangs in bearing: yet you shall crave to have your husband, and he shall master you" (Genesis 3:16). Every sin brings its own punishment, and the one who commits it tries to escape, but one cannot do so, because the One is just who says to man do not do so. Child carriage and birth would have been as joyous as connection and conception, if sin had not been permitted to come in. All pains are the result of sin whether of body or soul. It is however better to be punished in body, and have a chance to save the soul, than to be punished in body and lose the soul. Pain is dreadful, but remember sin is the cause.

## 28TH WEEK

### RESULTS OF THE FALL (Cont.)

(g) Cursed Earth. To the man He said, "Since you have listened to your wife and have eaten from the tree of which I forbade you to eat, cursed is the ground on your account, you shall win food from it with suffering all your life, thorns and thistles shall bear it for you, and you must eat plants of the field; in the sweat of your brow you must earn your food until you return to the ground from whence you were taken; for dust you are, and you shall return to dust" (Genesis 3:17-19). All human beings, but Adam and Eve, have known only the cursed earth. The beautiful world, that our heavenly Father gave our first parents, was never seen by any human eye, but the first two. He cursed the earth to save man. Man must suffer as long as he eats food from a cursed earth. Anything used from that which is cursed, is cursed itself, and the only way to make it a blessing is to ask the one who cursed it to bless it. Hence everything taken from the earth remains cursed, if our heavenly Father does not bless it at the request of those who ask. A cursed earth as beautiful as it is, what if we could have seen it before it was cursed. It was man's heaven and a beautiful one at that.

## 29TH WEEK

## RESULTS OF THE FALL (Cont.)

(h) Suffering. You shall win food from the ground with suffering all your life (Genesis 3:17). The suffering that has come upon humanity is indescribable. Everything he uses causes suffering to the human family one way or another. All the inventions produced by him, while blessing in part they also have caused intense suffering. Every day since man sinned and human beings have increased upon the earth, there has been and ever will be suffering. For man's sake everything that has life has felt this suffering. We are in a world of suffering. Men, women, children, animals of all kinds have felt, and are feeling, and will feel the fires of suffering. If it is not brought on by one thing it is by another. Man cannot escape this suffering which the Lord has placed upon him, a punishment for sin. For the human family to escape it, all must return to our Father and obey like Jesus.

## 30TH WEEK

## RESULTS OF THE FALL (Cont.)

(i) Thorns and Thistles. Thorns and thistles shall bear it for you (Genesis 3:18). Here we have a creation of thorns and thistles to fit a sinful world. A world without sin needs no thorns nor thistles, but a world where sin abounds needs them to remind man of the piercing sins that reside in the souls of men. Any time when one is not well protected as he walks in the midst of thorns and thistles, he is reminded that he must be clad himself so as to escape the pains inflicted by the piercing thorns and thistles. If one fails to clothe himself so as to escape the piercing of the pointed thorns and thistles, then he must suffer the painful results of their piercing the body. So also are the piercing pains of sin in the soul, when it is not properly protected by the garments from Jesus Christ. A body exposed to thorns and thistles is in much danger like the soul exposed to sin and Satan.

## 31ST WEEK

### RESULTS OF THE FALL (Cont.)

(j) Eat Plants. And you must eat plants of the field (Genesis 3:18). Man is now given a wider territory to get his food from, and instead of eating the fruit from the trees in the garden, he must eat the plants of the field. The Eternal planted for him to begin with, and all he had to do was to dress it and keep it; but now he must plant, till, dress and keep it himself. The plants coming from a cursed earth, being cursed also make the bodies sustained by them, continue in their cursed state, until they return to the cursed earth as they were before; and there remain until the earth, that was cursed, gets its regeneration in the day of its redemption (Genesis 3:19, Romans 8:19-21). The field is not as beautiful as the garden was, nor is its produce as good, nor as pleasant. He had a perfect garden in which he lived before, but he has an imperfect field that he lives in now and eats from.

## 32ND WEEK

### RESULTS OF THE FALL (Cont.)

(k) Earn Food by Sweat. In the sweat of your brow you must earn your food (Genesis 3:19). At first all man had to do was get his food from the fruit trees, but after he sinned, he must earn it, helping to keep in his mind the awfulness of sin. Each day as he toils in the heat of the sun, the hard tasks of labor caused him to sweat much, thus pulling out of his body through the pores of his skin much of the elements that go to make up his body.

Before he sinned the sun did not burn him, nor was his dressing and keeping the garden of such that it caused him to sweat. The whole program has changed, and man is the cause of it by believing what the devil said rather than God, his Creator.

## 33RD WEEK

## RESULTS OF THE FALL (Cont.)

(1) Death. But you must not eat of the tree that yield knowledge of good and evil, for on the day you eat from that tree you shall die (Genesis 2:17). The first death that came to man was spiritual. Spiritually he died the day he believed the devil. He was separated from God, which is death to any soul. This death came while he lived in his body. The man who was created with all the spiritual life necessary is now dead in trespasses and in sin, and in a place where his Creator has never been. All power to do himself any good is gone, and can only be gotten through another. (b) Physical Death. Until you return to the ground from which you were taken; for the dust you are, and you return to dust (Genesis 3:19). Adam lived hundreds of years after he died spiritually, before he died physically, but was slowly dying all the time until at last he passed from the earth as a living being. The twofold death came as was prophesied to him. All who disbelieve God's prophesy will some day experience the truth of it as did Adam and Eve.

## 34TH WEEK

## MAN'S REDEMPTION

**And I will put enmity between thee and the woman, and between thy seed and her seed; It shall bruise thy head, and thou shalt bruise his heel** (Genesis 3:15). This is the first expression made that brings out the idea of the triumph of Jesus Christ, that man might be redeemed from the stronghold of sin and Satan. While this was expressed to Satan through the serpent, by our Father, in condemnation for his acts, yet it was taught to Adam

# ONE YEAR'S STUDY ON MAN    61

and Eve by our Father. This was the first good news to man after the fall, and the beginning of God's grace and gospel for man's salvation. The seed of the woman was Jesus Christ, and the head of the serpent was the devil (Romans 16:20). This prophecy was fulfilled in the coming of Jesus in the human flesh, and conquering Satan in all that he had, to keep man from being redeemed.

## 35TH WEEK

### MAN'S REDEMPTION (Cont.)

The seed of the woman was not the woman's seed but the Son of God, using woman as the holder, carrier, and deliverer, in order that He would be wrapped in human flesh, that He might suffer as a man for men, but redeem men as God in human flesh. Wrapped in Genesis 3:15, is the Word of God that man's redemption would come at a time when the powers of hell through Satan could not prevent it. When this was made known to Adam and Eve they repented and believed our Father. Hence, Eve and Adam looked forward with eager eyes to see the fulfillment of the Word. Had our Father in His infinite love and mercy, not begun His grace for man, the first parents would have been lost entirely, Adam being the figure of Jesus Christ before the fall (Romans 5:14). Our Father loved him even though he did disobey Him, so much so, that He gave His Son as was promised to them in Eden.

## 36TH WEEK

### MAN'S REDEMPTION (Cont.)

Under the grace of God as being in Eden's Garden, is seen the great heart of our Father in the wonderful provisions made, and not after the physical death of Adam and Eve, but while they yet lived, giving them an opportunity to be saved as well as his posterity (Genesis 3:15). What a merciful Father is He. All of His dealings and expressions to Adam and Eve, are not expressed, but we have it all implied in what is expressed, and the one consecrated to Him wholly being a minister of the mysteries of God, the Holy Spirit will reveal to him all that he needs to know about it. His state was bad, and standing was worse, yet God had mercy on him, and gave him an opportunity to make good. How merciful! Our Father's goodness does not change because of man's attitude toward Him. Man fails but God never does. He proved all the above in life, and death of Jesus Christ upon earth. No man can know this goodness as shown to our first parents and still rebel against God.

## 37TH WEEK

### MAN'S REDEMPTION (Cont.)

And God the Eternal made tunics for the man and his wife, and clothed them (Genesis 3:21). Here is the first demonstration of animal life taken as a substitute that would be used for man until the coming of Jesus Christ; who would give his life a substitute for man. The first sacrifice offered was for Adam and Eve. Our Father Himself killed the animals, and clothed Adam and Eve in their skins. Demonstrating the kind of substitute that would be used for man until the coming of Jesus Christ; who would give his life a substitute for man. God killing the animal, and clothing Adam and Eve in their skins, was an ocular demonstration of God killing His Son, and clothing humanity in the righteousness of Jesus Christ for salvation. Everyone who comes before God in the final end must be wrapped in the righteousness of Jesus Christ or God will be a consuming fire to him or her. As Adam and Eve wre protected by the use of animal skin, so humanity is protected by the use of the righteousness of Jesus.

## 38TH WEEK

Genesis 3:21 is continued to be developed in this lesson. This verse shows that man could not even clothe himself after the fall but out of the wonderful provision made by our Father he is able to be clothed beginning with the first, (Adam and Eve) and

# ONE YEAR'S STUDY ON MAN

on to the last one that shall believe in Jesus. This verse gives proof to the salvation of Adam and Eve, and all of their posterity who would accept our Father's way to save man. He taught them by example how to offer unto Him the substituted sacrifices that He would accept in man's place; until Jesus Christ should die on the cross, the final substitute for man's redemption. They accepted all our Father taught them, and also taught it to their children. This is why Cain and Abel at the end of the week offered their sacrifices unto our Father. Cain's was rejected because he did not offer it as was taught. Abel's was offered as he was taught, and his faith caused him to reach the desired end, which was Jesus Christ the author and finisher of our faith.

## 39TH WEEK

### MAN'S REDEMPTION (Cont.)

Then said God the Eternal, man has become like one of us, to know good and evil. He may now reach his hand to the Tree of Life, also, and by eating of it live forever (Genesis 3:22). To live forever knowing good and evil is an eternal punishment to one who is not God. Every effort, on the part of our Father after the fall was for man's salvation. Men who are lost are lost because they will not accept the way provided for them. Man knowing good and evil puts him in a sorrowful condition. The man that knows evil although saved as to soul keeps him sorry, because that which he hates is always present. It may not be present in his soul, but he sees it everywhere he looks, and keeps burdened until complete redemption comes to all. Knowing good only keeps one happy, hence a world of good is heaven, and a world of evil is hell, and a world of good and evil makes one happy at times, and before the happiness is gone, good sorrow comes in. This is why we have a mixed joy and sorrow. In the midst of such a condition there is hope, because the Tree of Life still lives, and he or she, who puts forth his hand, and takes it into his or her being, shall live forever. We must be cast out of the world of good and evil by death, that we might live in a world of good only, like Adam and Eve.

## 40TH WEEK

### MAN'S REDEMPTION (Cont.)

So God the Eternal expelled him from the garden of Eden (Genesis 3:23). This expulsion was not for his damnation, but his salvation. It was not salvation of soul, for that is implied in Genesis 3:15, 21. It was for salvation of body, that the normal man could be saved. He did not expell him as one who hated him, but as the God and Father of those whom he loved. Jesus Christ was given to the world of sinners, not when He came into the world as a baby, but was given by His Father before Adam broke the law in the garden. While we were still in the loins of Adam before anyone was born unto him, Jesus was given, while the world of men was still in the human tree. He also loved the tree, and brought it to repentance and salvation. The way to save anything from that which will destroy it, is to separate it from it. His expulsion, from the garden that was thought by many to be a curse, was a blessing. In the infinite mercy, wisdom, and grace of our Father, Adam and Eve found salvation in Christ for themselves.

## 41ST WEEK

### MAN'S REDEMPTION (Cont.)

To till the ground from whence he had been taken (Genesis 3:23). As man goes to his field of labor day by day, he shows forth that obedience to divine command given him through our parents Adam and Eve. For our Father said to him, "In the sweat of your brow you must earn your food until you return to the ground" (Genesis 3:19). The constant tillage of the soil killing the vegetation and insects that hinder crop production, keep man ever reminded that some day he will go to the earth just as the grasses and plant-life of all kinds. The man, who tills the soil at the dictates of the Holy spirit, lives in the garden of God. All that our Father commands men to do is for their salvation. With joy he brings forth the labor of his hands, and with much thanksgiving

## ONE YEAR'S STUDY ON MAN 65

he consecrates his soul and body unto the Lord and lives in the joy and happiness of Eden. Let us go back to the farm life as of old.

### 42ND WEEK

### MAN'S REDEMPTION (Cont.)

He drove the man out, and set the cherubim at the east of the garden of Eden, with a blade of a sword which turned every way to keep the Tree of Life (Genesis 3:24). We come now to the established place to meet God the Eternal. He did not establish this place for man's damnation, but his salvation. Everyone who approached this place properly was accepted by Him. He taught the first parents how to come and in turn they taught their posterity. This was our Father's mercy seat where grace was displayed for man's redemption. This symbolic figure was a type of the Spirit of God with His Word which is the Spirit's sword. The Word turns every way like the blade of a great sword, not to destroy those who would come to the "Tree of Life," but to cut and destroy every root and destroy every root and branch of sin in the soul of everyone that took hold of the Tree of Life (Ephesians 6:17; Hebrews 4:12). It was a glad day with Adam, Eve and their posterity when our Father established the saving station for all who would come and be saved.

### 43RD WEEK

### MAN'S REDEMPTION (Cont.)

The "Tree of Life" in the midst of the garden, was a type of Jesus Christ (Genesis 2:9, 3:22; Revelation 2:7; 22:2, 14). This tree's fruit was for the healing of the nations. When rightly interpreted it is the words of Jesus Christ that heal. Anyone believing in His Words hath Eternal Life. The leaves represent the words of Jesus. Any nation that eats them will be healed of the disease of sin. Sin is the contagious disease of the soul, and can be healed only by the application of the blood of Jesus. The blood is applied only when one believes His Word. The flesh and blood of Jesus is the food and drink of every hungry and thirsty soul. Jesus expressed this in his discourse to his disciples (John 6:51-58).

## 44TH WEEK

### MAN IS REDEEMED FROM WHAT?

(1) The curse of the law (Galatians 3:13). Christ has redeemed us from the curse of the law by becoming a curse for us (Galations 3:13). The only way that man came from under the curse of the law is that he was redeemed by Jesus Christ. All who have believed in Him are rescued from under the curse of the law.

(2) From all iniquity. He gave Himself for us to redeem us from all iniquity (Titus 2:14). Every sin committed, and sins that come from omission, He has redeemed us from them all. No one needs to sin when he has been redeemed. From all compulsions to sin, man has been redeemed by Jesus Christ.

(3) From the house of bondage (Deuteronomy 13:5). The slave pen, in which Israel was held, was a type of sin in which everyone is held in bondage by Satan who has not been redeemed by Jesus Christ.

## 45TH WEEK

### REDEEMED FROM WHAT? (Cont.)

(4) From our enemies (Psalm 136:24). No enemy can do any more to the Christian man than our Father permits. Men, who are redeemed by the blood of Christ, should never fear an enemy.

(5) From Adversity (2 Samuel 4:9). That which men call adversity becomes a blessing to the redeemed of the Lord, and makes for Christian men, prosperity.

(6) From Trouble (Psalm 25:22). The redeemed man is free from trouble in the sense of its becoming a hindrance to him. Trouble is a helper to all of the redeemed, but we do not understand it as such until we are taught.

## ONE YEAR'S STUDY ON MAN

(7) From Distress (1 Kings 1:29). We are burdened and overcome by distress many times because we do not consider that we are redeemed from it. Distress cannot burden one who is taught that Christ has redeemed him from such.

(8) From deceit (Psalm 72:14). No one needs to lie about anything, deceiving the one who needs the truth. All deception comes from the devil. No redeemed man should be deceitful to anyone.

### 46TH WEEK

### REDEEMED FROM WHAT? (Cont.)

(9) From Destruction (Psalm 103:4). Every life that has the blood of Jesus applied to it is eternal. No destruction can come to him who is redeemed by our Saviour. All of the redeemed have their lives hidden with Christ in God, and there is no destruction in Him (Colossians 3:3).

(10) From Death (Hosea 13:14; Job 5:20). The world of the redeemed has been living in slavish fear of death ever since man fell. Men of the Christian faith, who have not been properly taught, are still in bondage to this thought. All believers in our Redeemer are freed from death forever. There is no life in death, and no death in the life of the redeemed.

(11) From the Grave (Psalm 49:16). No grave can hold the redeemed of our Father any more than it held the redeemer. Our bodies will only sleep there as though it was a night. The morning of the resurrection will tell the story of the weakness of the grave, and the strength of redemption.

### 47TH WEEK

### REDEEMED FROM WHAT? (Cont.)

(12) From Hell (Psalm 86:13). All that has been set up by Satan

and for Satan, the redeemed man has been delivered from by Christ Jesus. Anyone who goes to hell goes because he does not believe that Jesus went to hell for every man, and has redeemed every one that accepts Him from it. All who do not accept Him must go for themselves, and never be redeemed from it. All men who are redeemed from hell must be redeemed while living in the human body. No man is a real master who has not been redeemed. To be redeemed by Christ Jesus is to have the mastery over self, and all its lustful desires. He who is redeemed from lust, is redeemed from sin, and he who is redeemed from death, is redeemed from hell, and he who is redeemed from hell, is redeemed from that lake which burns with fire and brimstone (James 1:15).

## 48TH WEEK

### WHO REDEEMED MAN?

The Man Christ Jesus (Psalm 19:14; 78:34; Proverbs 23:11; Isaiah 41:14; 63:16). Man should be happy to take the place that Jesus has given him. Christ Jesus who gave redemption to man being a man Himself, he never lost one moment, nor allowed himself to let go one thing while on earth, that was to be used for the redemption of man. All men should be like the World's Redeemer. He gave His whole life as a man, that the world of men might be redeemed. Man should not withhold from His Redeemer anything that He asks him for, or fail to do anything He requires of him, seeing that the man Christ Jesus gave Himself a ransom for men. Know Him, believe Him and do what He says, because He is our Redeemer.

## 49TH WEEK

### MAN IS OUR FATHER'S GLORY (1 Corinthians 11:7)

Every man should consider himself highly honored to be the glory of our Father, so much so, that he should be happy to play his part as a master leader in all that our Father requires of him.

Each day should be filled with kind words, and loving deeds, looking forward to show the world that he is the glory of our Father. Having His nature puts out the same kind of fruit borne by His Son, our Redeemer. The man that knows in truth that he is our Father's glory, loves in a holy atmosphere that is glorious and grand. His presence shows forth, and reflects the light and life of the Son who is the only Redeemer of man. Being His glory, let us be glorious that all may see our Father truly.

## 50TH WEEK

## MAN BELONGS TO OUR FATHER

1st. By Creation (Genesis 1:27). Man should not be attracted by the creatures more than by the Creator. Since sin has entered into the world, to be attracted by creatures more than the Creator, it gives the devil a chance again to deceive, and to lead man entirely away from His Creator. No god should ever be thought of or worshipped by man, but his Creator. The creature man has no right to listen to, bow down before, or worship any other than the Creator whose instructions ring loud and clear to every man, from Genesis to Revelation, **"Thou shalt have no other gods before Me"** (Exodus 20:3). The Creator has a right to give rules and regulations to every creature of His hand whether things, angels or men. We are His by creation.

## 51ST WEEK

## MAN BELONGS TO OUR FATHER (Cont.)

2nd. By Redemption (Isaiah 41:14; 44:6; 60:16; 63:16). Every redeemed man should surrender all to our Father. His soul, body and spirit belong to Him because He redeemed them through His Son at an infinite price. It was blood that was paid for him, not human blood, nor the blood of animals, but the blood of Christ Jesus, the Divine Man (Matthew 26:28; 1 Corinthians 11:25; Ephesians 1-7; Colossians 1:20; Hebrews 9:12; 1 Peter 1:2). Any layman, who knows experientially that this was done for Him by Jesus, gives all to Him gladly, and becomes shouting happy that he is able to do so. Men only possess things, and want those things to be conformed to what they desire absolutely. Our Father owns men and should He not have absolute control over them? Men get what they possess from our Father, and want to be the only one to control. Our Father created and redeemed man using His best in creation and redemption for him. Let us read every command, and obey it acccording to the Spirit's teaching each day, for we are His by redemption.

## 52ND WEEK

Ye are an epistle of Christ, ministered by us, written not with ink, but with the Spirit of the Living God; not in tables of stone, but in tables that are hearts of flesh (1 Corinthians 33).

The Christian man must be a living Bible. He is our Father's master agent in the world. The Christian man must contain as much of Christ in his life as the Bible sets forth, in proportion as Christ brings Himself into him. The Bible points to Christ always. The Christian man's life must point to Christ always. The professed Christian that does not point to Christ in his life is not a Christian. Every word, sentence, paragraph, type, shadow, symbol, picture and everything that the Bible holds out points toward Christ. Man's words, acts, deeds and his very being should point to Christ, and if a Christian indeed will do so. The Christian man is the world's leader and he should hasten and take his place.

**SPECIAL FOR THE BROTHERHOOD UNION**

**THE HOLY SPIRIT**

This is not divided into weekly studies, but is left for each one who teaches, to cover that which he desires at each weekly meeting.

It may be studied by topics, using one for each week; or by paragraphs. Whatever method used, be sure it is mastered thoroughly.

Scriptures for devotions must be taken from the lesson taught each week. When many scriptures are given, use the one dictated by the Holy Spirit.

# THE HOLY SPIRIT

## I. His Deity

A—He is God. The source of our knowledge. (a) This comes to us through the dealings of Peter with Ananias and Sapphira (Acts 5:3, 4, 9). (b) Comes to us from Jesus Christ in His Spirit through Paul (1 Corinthians 3:16; 6:19; 12:4-6).

2. Who God is. (a) He is Spirit (John 4:24). (1) Unseeable and unknowable without Jesus Christ and in His Spirit (John 1:18; 6:46; Colossians 1:15; 1 Timothy 6:16; 1 John 4:12; 1 Corinthians 2:11). Being God, all pronouns, that are applied to the Father and Son are applied to Him, He is never said to be it, when properly referred to, but always He, Him, etc.

## II. His Personality

B—He is a Person. (1) His name appears with others who are persons. (a) He is spoken of as a person in the Great Commission (Matthew 28:29). (b) In the direct statement of Christ Himself (John 16:14). (c) In the statement made by the Apostles and older brothers to the gentile Brotherhood, (Acts 5:28). (d) He is classed with the Father and Son (2 Corinthians 13:14; Jude 21; 1 Peter 1:1, 2).

2. His Work is that of a Person. (a) His brooding upon the face of the waters, (Genesis 1:2) (b) His effort to save man (Genesis 6:3). (c) He is man's teacher (Luke 12:12). (d) He convicts the world (John 16:8). (e) Regenerates the soul (John 3:5). (f)Does as He wills (John 3:8). (g) Speaks through men (Acts 2:4). (h) Commands missionaries where to go and what to do (Acts 8:29; 10:19, 20; 16:6). 7. (i) Tells the church what to do (Acts 13:2). (j) Helps man and makes intercession for him (Romans 8:26). (k) Searches the deep things of Our Father (1 Corinthians 2:10, 11). (1) The Father giveth life through Him (Romans 8:11). (m) He gives gifts to Christians (1 Corinthians 12:8-11). (n) He moved men to write the Bible (2 Peter 1:21). (o) He sanctifies the Christians (2 Thessalonians

2:13; 1 Peter 1:2).

3. He is affected as persons are. (a) The rebellion of the people grieved Him (Isaiah 63:10; Ephesians 4:30. (b) He is resisted as a person (Acts 7:51).

### III. The Work Of The Holy Spirit In Man

A—For Regeneration (John 3:5-8); Titus 3:4-6). 1. Man's Part considered. (a) The unity of contrition, repentance and faith (Psalm 34:18; Acts 20:21). (1) These are put in many by the Holy Spirit: hence they are gifts from God for man's use (Ephesians 2:8; Acts 5:31; 11:18). (2) These gifts were all included in the Son of God (John 4:10). (b) Complete surrender to the Holy Spirit (Matthew 16:24-26).

In the consideration of man's part, we must not forget that it is only classed as man's part, on the ground of that which the Holy Spirit put in man to be used by him, as the fruit is put in the tree to be produced by it.

Man is helpless as to his salvation without Our Father. Therefore it is wholly a gift from Him (John 6:44, 45).

2. The Holy Spirit's part, apart from that which He put in man (John 3:5-8; Titus 3:4-6).

B—For Keeping Him. (1) To keep one from sin there must be in one the Holy Spirit, who is the keeper of man (2 Timothy 1:12-14). (2) When the Holy Spirit dwells in one, he knows it. (a) By loving Our Father (John 4:7-12). (b) By longing for Our Father (Psalm 42:1). (c) By longing for His commandments to keep them (Psalm 119:131; John 14:15). (d) By praying always like Jesus (Luke 6:12; Acts 2:42). (e) By hungering and thirsting after righteousness (Matthew 5:6). (f) By having a gift from Him (1 Corinthians 12:4-11). (g) By producing fruit like His (Galatians 5:22, 23). (h) By His being renewed each day like Jesus. (1) By increasing in wisdom and manliness in favor with God and man (Luke 2:52). Any one, who day by day brings God and man closer and closer, has the Holy spirit within him or her. There is not one thing in man that can do this, apart from the Holy Spirit that dwells in him. This

## THE HOLY SPIRIT

is known in the character of any one, and shown in the conduct of his or her life (1 John 2:6). (2) By not conforming to the present age, but by being transformed by the entire renewal of one's mind so that he or she may learn by experience what the will of Our Father is. That is all that is good and acceptable to Him (Romans 12:2).

One who does not have new experiences day by day from the work of the Holy Spirit within him or her cannot know the will of Our Father. One who does not know His will cannot do it. Our knowing it helps our doing it, and our doing it helps our knowing it (John 7:17). Knowledge is increased in both the physical and spiritual worlds by doing. Wisdom comes from Our Father through the prayer of faith (James 1:5). (3) The outward man or the body loses its hold on things natural day by day but the inward man, the spirit, gets a stronger hold on things spiritual day by day. One is dying (the body) while the other is getting more life (the spirit) each day. Dying things (the bodies) do not control living things (the spirit). No one who is being renewed in spirit lets the body control him: not even sometimes but at no time. This is not the work of man in body or spirit; but it is the work of the Holy Spirit in both (2 Corinthians 4:16; Romans 8:10). (4) To be renewed each day like Jesus, one must be renewed in the spirit of his or her mind, one must be clothed with the new man (Christ Jesus), who according to Our Father, has been formed in righteousness and Holiness of the Truth (Ephesians 4:23, 24). (5) Like Jesus, we are saved eternally. Not by anything we have done or could do, but by the appearing of Jesus Our Saviour in the world, coming specifically for that purpose, and the kindness of God Our Father. He saved us through the bath of regeneration which made us His own by this new birth; a change which cannot be changed again into the old nature and spirit of sin (Titus 3:5). Proceeding from this eternal salvation comes the mighty flow of "The Holy Spirit" within one who becomes a Fountain of Water springing up into Eternal Life. From this Fountain within one, there shall flow Rivers of Living Water (John 4:10; 7:38). These rivers of Living Water (The Holy Spirit) keeps one in continual process of a day by day renewal of the renewed.

## IV. What Makes This Regenerated Man Different From All Other Men.

A—He is begotten by God, the Holy Spirit. Being a son of The Holy One makes him created, conceived, nursed and birthed in the nature and Spirit of the Begetter (John 1:13; 3:5-8; 2 Corinthians 5:17-21; Galatians 6:15). These scriptures teach that we are begotten again into the likeness Our Father wants us, which likeness makes us like His Only begotten Son, who is the only one that is the God-Man.

We become a new Creation, which destroys our old nature and spirit; whereas we were subject to all that the devil wanted to make out of us before this creation; we are now in a state to be made all Our Heavenly Father wants to make us be. Inasmuch as in the old nature and spirit the devil could make us as bad as he wanted us to be, in the new nature and spirit Our Heavenly Father, for the sake of His Son, in Spirit, can make, and does make us, as good as He wants us to be when we trust Him for it (Matthew 12:33-35; Luke 6:45; Ephesians 2:10; Titus 2:14; 3 John 11).

The devil cannot tempt the children of God beyond the permission which God gives to him. Our Father never permits him to tempt us beyond the power of our advocate, Jesus Christ. All that he can do, he must get permission from Our Heavenly Father (Job 1st and 2nd chapters and Luke 22:31).

B—He lives in Christ. (a) The natural birth is a coming out of the body where it was conceived, for development and a continual growth of life's elements. The spiritual birth is the going into the body where it was conceived for a continual growth of that which is conceived, and the development of the Eternal Life given to the spirit (John 10:9; 15:4-7; 1 John 2:6; John 6:56).

Just as the natural seed is conceived in the body for its protection and growth, until the day of delivery into the world for its fuller growth and development; so the spirit of man is conceived in Jesus by the Holy Spirit for its protection and growth, until the day of redemption of the body, when it will be delivered into the eternal world for its ownership and joy of our Lord (Romans 8:21, 23; Colossians 3:2-4; Revelation 3:20).

# THE HOLY SPIRIT

The natural birth is coming out of the natural body into the world for growth, development and service. The spiritual birth is going into the Spirit of Jesus Christ for growth, development, protection and service.

For Christ to live is for all of His children to live. The only way to destroy a Christian is to destroy Christ, because we live, move, and have our being in Him. Since He is the greatest power in all existence, whether time or eternity, we are safe, living in the body or out of it. Because we are in Him, and no one can take us out of Him (John 14:20; Romans 6:11; 8:1; 14:7-9; 2 Corinthians 5:17).

The best protection any one has on earth is that which is given to the Christian in whom the Holy Spirit dwells. We are sealed and shielded from all danger from men, demons or the devil (2 Corinthians 1:22; Ephesians 1:13, 14). We were chosen in Him before the foundation of the world. Not as a mental picture in His mind as one would be in our minds, or an imagination, because whatever is in the mind of Our Father is real. He does not deal in fancies, but realities (Ephesians 1:4).

C—Christ Lives in Him. (a) Through what does Christ come into the regenerated man? It is through faith (Romans 5:1, 2; Ephesians 3:17). (b) In what does He come? He comes in His Spirit (Romans 5:5; Galatians 4:6; Titus 3:5, 6). (c) For what does He come? to become our life, and live thereafter for us, being Himself the fountain of life (Colossians 3:4; Galatians 2:20; John 1:4; 11:25).

The regenerated one living in Christ, and Christ living in him or her, makes his or her life eternal, because Christ is the Eternal Life (1 John 1:2; 2:25; 5:11, 13, 20). When He said I give unto my sheep that I know, and they hear my voice and follow me, He was not speaking about giving a part of Himself but the whole of Himself in His Spirit, because He is Eternal Life. Anyone living in Him and He in them, becomes what He is; that is why He says they shall never perish, because they cannot perish any more than He (John 10:28; 17:3).

The baby may perish, and die in its mother, but the Christian cannot perish and die in Christ. The same Spirit that begat and preserved Christ as a man, is the same Spirit that begets and

## THE HOLY SPIRIT

preserves the Christian (Matthew 12:18; Luke 4:18; John 3:34; Acts 1:2; 10:38). He does not beget and go away and leave that which he begets; but He dwells with the begotten, and supplies all the needs of him or her (John 14:16, 17, 23; John 15:7).

Weakness leaves when we by faith let Christ live within us. We with Christ are stronger than the devil, and can do all things through Him that He requires. Because He lives in us, we have more power within than the world has without (Philemon 4:13; 1 John 4:4).

Because of His Spirit within, the Christian, is the greatest power on the earth visible to the naked eye. It is through the Christian that Christ in His Spirit lives in the world, and that the world of sin must be destroyed, and the new heaven and new earth must be established.

It is Christ in His Spirit in the Christian that becomes his or her resurrection. (a) In the soul. (b) Of the body. The recreation of spirits and bodies of men will bring about the new heaven and new earth. Creation is waiting for its recreation, that is seen first in the spirit of the regenerated, and is in our day, and the days of all regenerated persons, whether past, present or future (John 5:21-26; Romans 8:19-23).

Christ in man destroyed all that the devil has done in him, through Adam, the first man created. He has bound Satan and spoiled all his good. We must not forget the devil is a conquered foe, and cannot touch the Christian without permission. Ever keep in mind that we are more than conquerors through Christ who lives in us in His Spirit (1 John 3:8; Matthew 12:24-29).

Any Christian that trusts God can get what is needed. The whole world of supply is open to him or her who trusts the Lord. Every temptation that the devil brings can be overcome by him or her who trusts it. Everyone that Christ lives in has an increase of faith each day for daily tasks and overcoming evil. Everyone that Christ in His Spirit dwells in, lives by faith and feeds on faithfulness (Mark 9:23; 1 Corinthians 10:13; 1 John 5:4; Habakkuk 2:4).

Faith is bound up in the hearts of those whom Christ lives in, and is ready for his or her use at any time. It is not bound up to

## THE HOLY SPIRIT

be bound, but it is bound in us as a reserve for usefulness when needed. Many Christians fail at times, because they do not use their faith when it is needed. When the Christian has Christ in His Spirit living within him or her, he or she has all that can be gotten for anything, health of body and of soul, strength and power for anything, life abundant, faith for more faith, hope for more hope, love for more love, and eternal life to be owned and controlled by him or her in all eternity (Matthew 9:29; 17:20; 21:21).

The double life of the Christian in Christ, and Christ in the Christian in His Spirit is a mystery, but it is eminently correct. The child formed in the womb of its mother with every element to make the man or the woman is a mystery also. Mysteries do not keep things from being true. There are mysteries all around and all about us, that cannot be understood by the finite mind; yet Our Father apprehends all, and reveals them to whom He will.

When the Holy Spirit begets the Christ Mind and spirit in the Christian, and the Christian in the Christ, He begets a holy, perfect being in character and elements like the Christ. Day by day these elements are developed into the likeness of Christ by the Holy Spirit from infancy (in Christianity) to childhood, from childhood to youthhood, from youthhood to manhood, from manhood to a full grown, well matured Christian (Hebrews 12:14; Ephesians 4:12, 23, 24; 2 Corinthians 13:9, 11; 1 Thessalonians 3:10; Philemon 3:15).

Perfection, in character and elements, does not mean completion in degrees. Many become confused with character, elements and degrees. Everyone knows that there are no imperfections in the Father, Son and Holy Spirit. Jesus Christ is the God-Man, who is the absolute perfect representation of the Trinity and humanity. He was begotten as such by the Holy Spirit, according to well directed plans brought on because of the foreknowledge and wisdom of the absolute perfection of the Deity. One perfectly holy in character, and absolutely perfect in elements, cannot beget one unlike Himself in character and elements. Inasmuch as one is begotten in Him in spirit, by the Holy Spirit, there should be no doubt in the mind of one who has been begotten by Him as to the perfection of character and elements of the begotten (Isaiah

9:6; John 8:46; 2 Corinthians 5:21; 1 Peter 1:19; Hebrews 7:26-28).

Inasmuch as Jesus Christ is the embodiment of holiness and perfection, all who are begotten of Him cannot be Jesus Christ, but must be like Him. He does not beget sinners, but Christians. He does not save in sin, but from sin. He does not beget grown Christians, but infant Christians, who will grow in His likeness. No one can grow in the likeness of one, who is not conceived, developed and born in that likeness (Hebrews 1:3; 1 John 5:20).

Christ in us is our hope of Glory. There can be no guarantee of salvation to the body, without perfection of spirit. The human body, with all its imperfections, must have a perfect spirit developing within it to assure it its salvation. Had Jesus Christ not been absolutely perfect, He could not have saved the world of sinners. No one, living in sin in the inmost recesses of his spirit, can be an agent to work with Jesus Christ in His Spirit, for the salvation of sinners. Christ may work him, but He does not work with him (Colossians 1:27; 1 John 1:7; Revelation 1:5; 5:9; Mark 16:20; 1 Corinthians 3:9; 2 Corinthians 6:1; 1 John 2:1, 2).

The old creation is imperfect, but the recreation is perfect in its nature and character. The seed of the corn is imperfect when it is compared with any portion of it in its developing state; and is very imperfect when it is compared with it in the ear. When it is compared with it in the full grain in the ear, it is more imperfect. When it is compared with it when the grain has reached its perfect state in the ear, it is most imperfect.

But when the seed corn is compared with another seed of its same kind identically, then it is perfect. When its growth is compared with each proportionate part as it grows, it is perfect, even unto the perfect state in the ear. The above illustration shows the difference in degrees, although the same in kind.

When there is imperfection in the nature and character of anything, regardless to its development, there will be imperfection in its growth. When there is imperfection in its growth, there will be imperfection in the completion of its growth. To have a complete perfect growth at maturity, there must be perfection in the seed, and each degree of its growth (Matthew 7:18; 12:33;

# THE HOLY SPIRIT

Luke 6:45).

To be a grain of corn to begin with, there must be a grain or grains of corn to end with. It is impossible to be corn in nature and kind to begin with, and not be cotton in nature and kind to end with. There can be no blending of seed so as to grow half corn, and half cotton in nature and kind. The command from Our Father is for each seed to bring forth its kind (Genesis 1:11, 12).

A like comparison is made here of those who are in Christ, and Christ in them. When we are first begotten of Our Father, in His Son, through His Spirit, we are imperfect when we are compared with the likeness of the man, Christ Jesus, in His growing and developing state. And we are more imperfect when we are compared with Him in His grown state; and most imperfect when compared to Him in His full grown state, and out of comparison with Him in His Absolute state, in which He becomes the express image of the Deity.

But when we are compared with Him in His conceived and begotten state as an infant, as to nature and kind, we are perfect, because the same One that begat Him, who is the Christ, is the same One that begat the Christian to be like Him. God the Father, God the Son, and God the Holy Spirit cannot through the Holy Spirit beget an imperfect being in nature and kind. Every Christian, begotten of Our Father through His Spirit, is a gift from Our Father to the world of sinners for their salvation; as well as every pastor called and sent by Our Father is a gift from Our Father to the church, for its continued perfection in Christ (James 1:17; Jeremiah 3:15; Ephesians 4:11-13).

If there is not anything in us to begin with like Christ, there cannot be anything in us to end with like Him. Whatever that is in us that makes us like Him to end with, that is the same thing that is perfect in us, that does not differ in nature and kind, as we grow only in degree. To deny holiness of character in nature and kind in its perfect elements, is to deny the regenerating or recreating work of Jesus Christ, in His Spirit, in the hearts of men, for their salvation, and the salvation of the world, through those who are begotten of Our Father for that purpose. The law of making good is to make the source good of anything (Matthew 7:15-20;

**84**  **THE HOLY SPIRIT**

James 3:12).

Do not let sin deceive to the end that we will believe, and teach contrary to the Word and Spirit of Jesus Christ. Because we do not understand it all, let us not deny the possibility of it, as done by Jesus Christ in His Spirit. We know to be perfect to begin with, to grow or to end with, is impossible for a sinful human being. And it is just as impossible as it is for one to save him or herself, (Romans 7:14-24).

Perfection in any body is not the work of man; but is wholly the work of Jesus Christ in His spirit in man, and whatever He does is perfect. The Holy Spirit is able to make man anything Christ wants him to be, if only the man will faith it. All the ground the ancient Israelite puts his foot on in Canaan was given him, and all the elements of righteousness the modern Christian puts his faith on is his (Romans 7:25; Deuteronomy 11:25; Joshua 1:3).

Christ is not in the one, nor is that one in Christ, who professes to be a Christian, and in him or her there is no holiness of nature, or perfection of character (Romans 6:4; 2 Corinthians 5:17; Galatians 6:15).

We are not conceived by imperfect beings, nor are we begotten by imperfect beings. We have not an imperfect standard to be measured by and grow like. In our regenerated spirits, we are not placed in an imperfect being for our sustenance, protection and growth. We are not given imperfect food to appease our hunger, nor imperfect water to quench our thirsty souls. But we are conceived, begotten and measured by an absolute perfect standard; placed in an absolute perfect being for our sustenance, protection and growth. We are given absolutely perfect food to appease our hunger, and absolutely perfect water to quench our thirsty spirits, which is Jesus Christ, the True God and eternal Life. And we are commanded to abide in Him, and He will abide in us, while the changing ages roll on, He will never change; but abide forever. Hence we are saved, and safe in Him, who is the Perfection of The Deity (Leviticus 11:44; 19:2; 20:7; Matthew 5:48; Hebrews 12:14; John 15:4; John 10:28).

V—Christ In The Christian and the Christian In Christ, Fits Him or Her to be Guided by the Holy Spirit Like the Christ.

## THE HOLY SPIRIT

The Man Christ Jesus did not go anywhere, or do anything, as a man, without the direction and leadership of the Holy Spirit. He did not start out on His mission until He was anointed by Him. Nor did He enter the wilderness, to be tempted by the devil without Him. While in the wilderness forty days and nights being tempted by the devil, He was led by the Holy Spirit in every temptation, until those days ended (Matthew 3:16; Mark 1:10; Luke 3:22; Matthew 4:1; Mark 1:12; Luke 4:1).

Inasmuch as He was directed and led by the Holy Spirit, setting the example for every Christian, then you know we cannot do anything without Him. Being the God-man, He could have made it well without the Holy Spirit, but He would not have been an example for us, who are not, and could not be God-men.

This was also proven in His expression to the disciples when He said, . . . **tarry ye in Jerusalem until ye be endued with power from on high,** Luke 24:49. Many individual persons, ministers, and churches have failed, because they have attempted to live, and do the work of Our Father without the Holy spirit. All the work of Jesus Christ in the world, must be done according to the direction and power of the Holy Spirit. The work of redemption belongs to Our Father, through the God-man Jesus Christ in His Spirit (Genesis 3:15, Romans 3:20-30; Colossians 1:13, 14).

Inasmuch as we could not redeem ourselves, we ought not attempt to keep ourselves in anything. Every powerful minister and church is filled with the Holy Spirit. The power of the minister and the church is the Holy Spirit. The church of Christ, and the ministry of Christ have not and cannot lose their power. The church, in its reality, is able to do today what it did on the day of Pentecost and forward. The real line of Christ's ministry has not been broken. Many places a mountain range runs low but is mountain just the same (John 14:16, 17, 26).

Because many churches, and ministers have not been guided by the Holy spirit, that does not say the church and minister, builded on Christ, have lost their power. It takes power for the church to conquer hell, and bring out of the kingdom of darkness the captives that are prisoners, into the kingdom of Our Father's Son. His declaration which cannot be changed gives us the eternal thought

(Matthew 16:18).

The gospel of Christ must be preached like He preached it. And this can only be done by the church and minister, who are filled like "The Man, Christ Jesus, with the Holy Spirit." No minister need think he can beat Jesus Christ. The Holy Spirit fits him for the ministry of Christ Jesus. The secular schools of the land, all of them combined together, cannot fit anyone with the power to preach, and teach the Gospel of Christ.

For one to carry out the ministry of the Man Christ Jesus, he must be trained in the School of Christ. Schools that call themselves Divinity Schools that are not filled with the Spirit of Jesus Christ are but institutions for the dwelling place of the devil.

The men and women who are trained in the School of Christ, keep Christ uppermost in their minds Instead of preaching and teaching the lives of those called heroes and great philosophers, their hearts are filled to the overflowing with the Word and Spirit of "That Man, Christ Jesus." And they preach, and teach like He did under the guidance and direction of the Holy Spirit (Luke 4:14-20; Job 5:13; Jeremiah 8:9; Matthew 11:25; Isaiah 29:14; 1 Corinthians 1:19-31; 2:6-9; 3:18-21; 2 Corinthians 1:12).

Men, who live in the thoughts of their minds according to the direction of the flesh are not in Christ; nor is Christ in them; nor are they led by the Holy Spirit. The failure to be in Christ, shows that one is not a Christian. No one can have the Spirit of "The Christ" and not be a Christian, neither can anyone be a Christian, and not have His spirit. Christians cannot live in the flesh, nor can sinners live in the Spirit.

Sinners do not delight in the Spirit, nor do Christians delight in the flesh. The mind of the flesh is the body through which the devil operates. The mind of the Spirit is the body through which Christ operates. The mind of the flesh is death, and the mind of the spirit is life.

The purpose for which Christ came in the flesh was to condemn sin in the flesh, so that the requirements of the law would be fulfilled in each Christian. There can be no disappointment to anyone who lives in the Spirit of "The Christ" (Romans 8:1-9).

To be born rightly and taught wrongly, brings on an entangle

## THE HOLY SPIRIT

ment that is hard to untangle. To have a perfect birth, and to be fed on imperfect food, hinders the growth, and stunts one to the end that he cannot be strong in the power of Our Father's might. Anyone who preaches and teaches that men, women, boys and girls, who are born of the spirit of God cannot be perfect in that which Our Father brings them into by His Spirit, day by day, is a hindrance to the Kingdom of God (Matthew 23:13-35).

All who live in sin are dead to the righteousness of our Father. All who live in righteousness are dead to sin. Christ, in His Spirit, does not dwell in sinners. The dwelling place of the Holy Spirit must be holy, not from without only, but from within as well— body and soul (Romans 8:6, 12, 13; 1 Corinthians 3:16, 17).

VI—The Completion of the Work of Redemption is in His Hands.

No one can be Spirit filled and not Spirit guided. Wherever He dwells He rules, and His rulership is according to the will of Our Father. He has all the work of the Deity in His hands, but He uses men whom He prepares as agents through which He works. All of Our Father is in the Holy Spirit. All of the Son is in the Holy Spirit. All of the Holy Spirit is in the Father. All of the Holy Spirit is in the Son. The Holy spirit is God the Father and Son, in the world continuing and bringing to completion the work of redemption for man's soul and body, and creation itself (John 16:7-15; Acts 1:7, 8).

**A BOOK ON**

**CHRISTIAN GIVING**

**AND**

**PAYING TITHES**

## GIVING

## I. INTRODUCTION

Everything that man has is a gift from Our Father. Man's body and spirit, and all that our eyes can behold, and all that our minds can think of, are gifts from Him. Surely creatures, who have received all from Him, are willing to give back to Him by giving to others and His cause, as He commands.

The Spirit of Our Father is seen in giving. All who will not give prove that they are not children of His, because He is the very embodiment of giving. His best was given to man, the greatest of which were His Son and the Holy Spirit.

No one can be a Christian who does not give as commanded. The Father, Son, and Holy Spirit gave all to man, and all who are born again have the same kind of Spirit that the Trinity has. All who fail are not His. The Bible of His Word teaches us to give in both the Old and New Covenants, which are essentially one.

## II. To Whom We Should Give

(a) To God Our Father. And this they did, not as we hoped, but first gave their own selves to the Lord, and unto us by the will of God (2 Corinthians 8:5). Neither yield ye your members as instruments of unrighteousness unto sin: but yield yourselves unto God, as those that are alive from the dead, and your members as instruments of righteousness unto God (Romans 6:13). (b) To the poor. He that hath pity upon the poor lendeth unto the Lord; and that which he hath given will he pay him again (Proverbs 19:17). Jesus said unto him, If thou wilt be perfect, go and sell that thou hast, and give to the poor, and thou shalt have treasures in heaven: and come and follow me (Matthew 19:21). (c) To the needy. And all that believed were together, and had all things common; and sold their possessions and goods, and parted them to all men, as every man had need (Acts 2:44, 45). But whoso hath this world's good, and seeth his brother have need, and shutteth up his bowels of compassion from him, how dwelleth the love of

God in him? (1 John 3:17). (d) To him that asketh. Give to him that asketh thee, and from him that would borrow of thee turn not thou away (Matthew 5:42). (e) To the house of the Lord. Now I have prepared with all my might for the house of my God the gold for things to be made of gold, and the silver for things of silver, and the brass for things of brass, the iron for things of iron, and wood for things of wood; onyx stones, and stones to be set, glistering stones, and of divers colours, and all manner of precious stones, and marble stones in abundance (1 Chronicles 29:2). And some of the chief of the fathers, when they came to the house of the Lord which is at Jerusalem, offered freely for the house of God to set it up in his place (Ezra 2:68).

### III. Who Should Give

(a) Christians rich and poor. And Jesus sat over against the treasury, and beheld how the people cast money into the treasury: and many that were rich cast in much. And there came a certain poor widow, and she threw in two mites, which make a farthing. And he called unto his disciples, and saith unto them, Verily I say unto you, That this poor widow hath cast more in, than all they which have cast into the treasury: For all they did cast in of their abundance; but she of her want did cast in all that she had, even all her living (Mark 12:41-44). (b) Everyone. Upon the first day of the week let every one of you lay by him in store, as God hath prospered him, that there be no gatherings when I come (1 Corinthians 16:2).

### IV. What We Should Give

(a) Self. And this they did, not as we hoped, but first gave their own selves to the Lord, and unto us by the will of God (2 Corinthians 8:5). This giving of self includes: (1) The heart. My son, give me thine heart, and let thine eyes observe my ways (Proverbs 23:26). (2) The mind. And thou shalt love the Lord thy God with all thy heart, and with all thy soul, and with all thy mind, and with all thy strength, this is the first commandment (Mark 12:30). (3)

## CHRISTIAN GIVING, PAYING TITHES 93

Attention and heed. Therefore we ought to give the more earnest heed to the things which we have heard, lest at any time we should let them slip (Hebrews 2:1). (4) Thanks. O give thanks unto the Lord; call upon His name: make known his deeds among the people (Psalm 105:1). Praise ye the Lord. O give thanks unto the Lord; for he is good: for his mercy endureth for ever (Psalm 106:1). O give thanks unto the Lord, for he is good: for his mercy endureth for ever (Psalm 107:1). O give thanks unto the Lord, for he is good: because his mercy endureth forever (Psalm 118:1). O, give thanks unto the Lord; for he is good: for his mercy endureth for ever (Psalm 136:1). (5) Talent. Heal the sick, cleanse the lepers, raise the dead, cast out devils: freely ye have received, freely give (Matthew 10:8). (6) Material needed. And the Lord spake unto Moses, saying, Speak unto the children of Israel, that they bring me an offering: . . . And this is the offering which ye shall take of them; gold, and silver, and brass, and blue, and purple, and scarlet, and fine linen, and goat's hair, and ram's skins dyed red, and badgers' skins, and shittim wood, oil for the light, spices for anointing oil, and for sweet incense, onyx stones, and stones to be set in the ephod, and in the breastplate. And let them make me a sanctuary; that I may dwell among them (Exodus 25:1-8). (7) Water. And whosoever shall give to drink unto one of these little ones a cup of cold water only in the name of a disciple, verily I say unto you, he shall in no wise lose his reward (Matthew 10:42). (8) Substance. Honour the Lord with thy substance, and with the firstfruits of all thine increase (Proverbs 3:9). (9) The first of the firstfruits of the ground. The first of the firstfruits of thy land thou shalt bring into the house of the Lord (Exodus 23:19). (10) Precious stones. And they with whom precious stones were found gave them to the treasure of the house of the Lord, by the hand of Jehiel the Gershonite (1 Chronicles 29:8). (11) Such as you have. But rather give alms of such things as ye have; and, behold, all things are clean unto you (Luke 11:41). For if there be first a willing mind, it is accepted according to that a man hath, and not according to that he hath not (2 Corinthians 8:12). (12) Fruit of your lips. By him therefore let us offer the sacrifice of praise to God continually, that is, the fruit of our lips giving thanks to his name (Hebrews 13:15). (13) Time. **Six days shalt thou labour, and do all thy work: but the seventh day is the sabbath of the Lord thy God: in it thou shalt not do any work, thou, nor thy son, nor thy daughter, thy manservant, nor thy maid-servant, nor thy cattle, nor thy stranger that is within thy gates** (Exodus 20:9, 10).

(a) Give as commanded. **Give, and it shall be given unto you; good measure, pressed down, and shaken together, and running over, shall men give into your bosom. For with the same measure that ye mete withal it shall be measured to you again** (Luke 6:38). (b) Work. Let him that stole steal no more: but rather let him labour, working with his hands the thing which is good, that he may have to give to him that needeth (Ephesians 4:28). (c) Sow plenty. But this I say, **he which soweth sparingly shall reap also sparingly; and he which soweth bountifully shall reap also bountifully** (2 Corinthians 9:6). (d) Sell what you have. Jesus said unto him, If thou wilt be perfect, go and sell that thou hast, and give to the poor, and thou shalt have treasure in heaven: and come and follow me (Matthew 19:21). Sell that ye have, and give alms; provide yourselves bags which wax not old, a treasure in the heavens that faileth not, where no thief approacheth, neither moth corrupteth. For where your treasure is, there will your heart be also (Luke 12:33, 34). (e) Be inspired by those who give. For I know the forwardness of your mind, for which I boast of you to them of Macedonia, that Achaia was ready a year ago; and your zeal hath provoked very many (2 Corinthians 9:2). (f) Lay by in store. Upon the first day of the week let every one of you lay by him in store, as God hath prospered him, that there be no gatherings when I come (1 Corinthians 16:2).

### V. How Much To Give

(a) Plenty. Give, and it shall be given unto you; good measure, pressed down, and shaken together, and running over, shall men give into your bosom. For with the same measure that ye mete it shall be measured to you again (Luke 6:38). (b) Tenth. And Melchizedek king of Salem brought forth bread and wine: and he

## CHRISTIAN GIVING, PAYING TITHES

was the priest of the most high God. And he blessed him, and said, Blessed be Abram of the most high God, possessor of heaven and earth: And blessed be the most high God, which hath delivered thine enemies into thy hand. And he (Abraham) gave him tithes of all (Genesis 14:18, 20). And Jacob vowed a vow, saying, If God will be with me, and will keep me in this way that I go, and will give me bread to eat, and raiment to put on, So that I come again to my father's house in peace; then shall the Lord be my God: And this stone, which I have set for a pillar, shall be God's house: and of all that thou shalt give me I will surely give the tenth unto thee (Genesis 28:20-22). And behold, I have given the children of Levi all the tenth in Israel for an inheritance, for their service which they serve, even the service of the tabernacle of the congregation in Israel (Numbers 18:21). Will a man rob God? Yet ye have robbed me. But ye say, Wherein have we robbed thee? In tithes and offerings. Ye are cursed with a curse: for ye have robbed me, even this whole nation (Malachi 3:8, 9). Woe unto you, scribes and Pharisees, hypocrites! for ye pay tithe of mint and anise and cummin, and have omitted the weightier matters of the law, judgment, mercy, and faith: these ought ye to have done, and not to leave the other undone (Matthew 23:23).

(a) When and through whom was it instituted? It was instituted by our Father in Abraham's time and through Abraham (Genesis 14:20). Abraham gave the tithe to Melchizedek, the only priest that represented the priesthood of Christ. Hebrews, 7th chapter. Inasmuch as Melchizedek was the representative of Christ, Abraham paid tithes to Jesus through him. The tithe is holy like the Sabbath, hence it belongs to our Father (Leviticus 27:30-32). Every holy thing belongs to Him, things, beasts, flocks, herbs and people. To withhold from Him His own when he asks for it is a sin.

The tithe was not instituted in the law that passed away when Christ came, and completed the plan of redemption, but was instituted in the gospel that was seen and participated in by Abraham through faith. This law was fulfilled by Christ, and is for all time (Matthew 5:17). The Levitical priesthood that received the tithes from the people, also paid the tithes through Levi in Abraham, when Abraham paid the tithes to Melchizedek (Hebrews

**96**            **CHRISTIAN GIVING, PAYING TITHES**

7:9, 10). This was before the Levites were born, or the law that passed away when they ceased, had been given, showing that the tithes were not instituted when this law was given that it might cease with it. All of the Levitical Priesthood law was imperfect, and gave way for the institution of the perfect law which came under the priesthood of Jesus Christ that was represented by Melchizedek before the Levitical priesthood. The Levitical priesthood had a law and priests subject to changes. The priesthood of Christ represented by Melchizedek was perpetual in time and eternity. It had no father nor mother, no beginning of days nor end of life, no change in time or eternity (Hebrews 7:1-3, 14-28). Inasmuch as Christ is unchangeable so also are all principles instituted in His government. Many teach it is not to be paid today because it was instituted in the Old Testament. Everything in God's creation and redemption, had its origin in the Old Testament (Proverbs 1:9). God our Father, God His Son, and God the Holy Spirit are all Old Testament persons. All that did not have its origin written in the Old Testament is not in existence. The tithe makes the poor equal to the rich in paying into the church. When the rich pays his tithes out of his millions and the poor pays his out of his poverty, he is equal to him with Our Father. Our Father's plan, in the Bible of His Word on giving and paying, is the best in all the world. It satisfies the giver and blesses both the giver and receiver. In all ages, those who have paid their tithes as commanded, have been blessed as promised to all who would do so. Abraham believed Our Father and it was counted to him for righteousness (Romans 4:3). Abraham is father of the faithful, but not the Father who begat us, because Our Father, through His Son in His Spirit, is the only one who begets. Abraham is the father of the called out as to faith. This idea implies the church which is the body of Christ. He was the first to get out from his father's house, from among his kindred and from his country, a similar thing that all must do who constitute the church, the body of Christ. Since He represents the church, and paid tithes to Melchizedek, who represented Jesus Christ, makes it binding upon the church to pay its tithes always. When the members of the church pay their tithes to the church, the called out, or the body of Christ, and

# CHRISTIAN GIVING, PAYING TITHES

its purpose in the world is to extend the Kingdom of Christ to earth's remotest bounds, the church in turn is compelled to pay its tithes for Kingdom building. Accepting Abraham's faith makes us accept his plan of paying the tithes also. Both Testaments teach us to pay tithes (Genesis 14:20, 28:22; Leviticus 27:30-32; Nehemiah 10:37; Malachi 3:8-10; Deuteronomy 23:23; Leviticus 11:42, 18:12; Hebrews 7:4-10).

## VI. When To Give

(a) First of the week. Upon the first day of the week let every one of you lay by him in store, as God hath prospered him, that there be no gatherings when I come (1 Corinthians 16:2). (b) Before it is needed. Therefore I thought it necessary to exhort the brethren, that they would go before unto you, and make up beforehand your bounty, whereof ye had notice before, that the same might be ready, as a matter of bounty, and not as of covetousness (2 Corinthians 9:5). (c) As we have an opportunity. As we have therefore opportunity, let us do good unto all men, especially unto them who are of the household of faith (Galatians 6:10). (d) While you have it. Say not unto thy neighbour Go, and come again, and to morrow I will give; when thou hast it by thee (Proverbs 3:28).

## VII. How To Give

(a) As the Lord has blessed you. And thou shalt keep the feast of weeks unto the Lord thy God with a tribute of a free-will offering of thine hand, which thou shalt give unto the Lord thy God (Deuteronomy 16:10). (b) As you have purposed. Let each man do according as he has purposed in his heart (2 Corinthians 9:7). (c) As you are able. Every man shall give as he is able, according to the blessing of the Lord thy God which He hath given thee (Deuteronomy 16:17). (d) Willing. Speak unto the children of Israel, that they bring me an offering: of every man willing that giveth it, ye shall take my offering (Exodus 25:2). And they came, every one whose heart stirred him up, and every one whom his spirit made willing, and they brought the Lord's offering, to the work of the tabernacle of the congregation, and for all his service, and for the holy garments (Exodus 35:21). I know also, my God, that thou triest the heart, and hast pleasure in uprightness. As for me, in the uprightness of my heart I have willingly offered all these things: and now have I seen with joy thy people, which are present here, to offer willingly unto thee (1 Chronicles 29:17). And some of the chief of the fathers, when they came to the house of the Lord which is at Jerusalem, offered freely for the house of God to set it up in his place (Ezra 2:68). For if there be first a willing mind, it is accepted according to that a man hath, and not according to that he hath not (2 Corinthians 8:12). (e) Liberally. How that in a great trial of affliction the abundance of their joy and deep poverty abounded unto the riches of their liberality (2 Corinthians 8:2). Being enriched in every thing to all bountifulness, which causeth through us thanksgiving to God. For the administration of this service not only supplieth the want of the saints, but is abundant also by many thanksgivings unto God; Whiles by the experiment of this ministration they glorify God for your professed subjection unto the gospel of Christ, and for your liberal distribution unto them, and unto all men (2 Corinthians 9:11-13). (f) **For to their power, I bear record, yea, and beyond their power they were willing of themselves** (2 Corinthians 8:3). (g) Cheerfully. **Every man according as he purposeth in his heart, so let him give; not grudgingly, or of necessity: for God loveth a cheerful giver** (2 Corinthians 9:7). (h) According to your ability. They gave after their ability unto the treasury of the work three score and one thousand drams of gold, and five thousand pounds of silver, and one hundred priest's garments (Ezra 2:69). (h) In Jesus' name. For whosoever shall give you a cup of water to drink in my name, because ye belong to Christ, verily I say unto you, he shall not lose his reward (Mark 9:41).

### VIII. How Not To Give

Grudgingly or of necessity. **Every man according as he purposeth in his heart, so let him give; not grudgingly, or of necessity;**

# CHRISTIAN GIVING, PAYING TITHES

for God loveth a cheerful giver (2 Corinthians 9:7). What not to do about giving, and why not to do it. **But a certain man named Ananias, with Sapphira his wife, sold a possession, and kept back part of the price, his wife also being privy to it, and brought a certain part, and laid it at the apostles' feet. But Peter said, Ananias, why hath Satan filled thine heart to lie to the Holy Ghost, and to keep back part of the price of the land? Whiles it remained, was it not thine own? and after it was sold, was it not in thine own power? why hast thou conceived this thing in thine heart? thou hast not lied unto men, but unto God. And Ananias hearing these words fell down, and gave up the ghost: and great fear came on all them that heard these things. And the young men arose, wound him up, carried him out, and buried him. And it was about the space of three hours after, when his wife, not knowing what was done, came in. And Peter answered unto her, Tell me whether ye sold the land for so much? And she said, Yea, for so much. Then Peter said unto her, How is it that ye have agreed together to tempt the Spirit of the Lord? behold, the feet of them which have buried thy husband are at the door, and shall carry thee out. Then fell she down straightway at his feet, and yielded up the ghost: and the young men came in and found her dead, and, carrying her forth, buried her by her husband. And great fear came upon all the church, and upon as many as heard these things** (Acts 5:1-11).

### IX. Reasons We Should Give

(a) Because we are God's stewards. **But thou shalt remember the Lord thy God: for it is he that giveth thee power to get wealth, that He may establish his covenant which He sware unto thy fathers, as it is this day** (Deuteronomy 8:18). **But who am I, and what is my people, that we should be able to offer so willingly after this sort? for all things come of thee, and of thine own have we given thee. For we are strangers before thee, and sojourners, as were all our fathers: our days on the earth are as a shadow, and there is none abiding. O Lord our God, all this store that we have prepared to build thee an house for thine holy name cometh**

**CHRISTIAN GIVING, PAYING TITHES**

of thine hand, and is all thine own (1 Chronicles 29:14-16). **Every man also to whom God hath given riches and wealth, and hath given him power to eat thereof, and to take his portion, and to rejoice in his labour; this is the gift of God** (Ecclesiastes 5:19). **The silver is mine, and the gold is mine, saith the Lord of hosts** (Haggi 2:8). **For the kingdom of heaven is as a man traveling into a far country, who called his own servants, and delivered unto them his goods** (Matthew 25:14). **Charge them that are rich in this world, that they be not high minded, nor trust in uncertain riches, but in the living God, who giveth us richly all things to enjoy** (1 Timothy 6:17). **As every man hath received the gift, even so minister the same one to another, as good stewards of the manifold grace of God** (1 Peter 4:10). (b) It honors God. **Honour the Lord with thy substance, and with the firstfruit of all thine increase** (Proverbs 3:9). (c) Out of gratitude to Christ for what He did. **For ye know the grace of our Lord Jesus Christ, that, though he was rich, yet for your sakes he became poor, that ye through his poverty might be rich** (2 Corinthians 8:9). (d) It is given as a trust fund to us. **And he spake a parable unto them, saying, The ground of a certain rich man brought forth plentifully: And he thought within himself, saying, What shall I do, because I have no room where to bestow my fruits? And he said, This will I do: I will pull down my barns, and build greater; and there will I bestow all my fruits and my goods. And I will say to my soul, Soul, thou hast much goods laid up for many years; take thine ease, eat, drink, and be merry. But God said unto him, Thou fool, this night thy soul shall be required of thee: then whose shall those things be, which thou hast provided? So is he that layeth up treasure for himself, and is not rich toward God** (Luke 12:16-21). Also Luke 19:12-26. (e) Because we are commanded to give **Give, and it shall be given unto you; good measure, pressed down, and shaken together, and running over, shall men give into your bosom. For with the same measure that ye mete withal it shall be measured to you again** (Luke 6:38). **Woe unto you, scribes and Pharisees, hypocrites! for ye pay tithe of mint and anise and cummin, and have omitted the weightier matters of the law, judgment, mercy and faith: these ought ye to have done,**

## CHRISTIAN GIVING, PAYING TITHES

and not to leave the other undone (Matthew 23:23). **Upon the first day of the week let every one of you lay by him in store, as God hath prospered him, that there be no gatherings when I come** (1 Corinthians 16:2). (f) It brings God's blessings to us. **Bring ye all the tithes into the storehouse, that there may be meat in mine house, and prove me now herewith, saith the Lord of hosts, if I will not open you the windows of heaven, and pour you out a blessing, that there shall not be room enough to receive it. And I will rebuke the devourer for your sakes, and he shall not destroy the fruits of your ground; neither shall your vine cast her fruit before the time in the field, saith the Lord of hosts. And all nations shall call you blessed: for ye shall be a delightsome land, saith the Lord of hosts** (Malachi 3:10-12). (g) His house needs it. **Speak unto the children of Israel, that they bring me an offering: of every man that giveth it willingly with his heart ye shall take my offering. And this is the offering which ye shall take of them; gold, and silver, and brass. And let them make me a sanctuary; that I may dwell among them** (Exodus 25:2, 3, 8). **And some of the chief of the fathers, when they came to the house of the Lord which is at Jerusalem, offered freely for the house of God to set it up in his place** (Ezra 2:68). (h) That we might be an example to others. **For I know the forwardness of your mind, for which I boast of you to them of Macedonia, that Achaia was ready a year ago; and your zeal hath provoked very many** (2 Corinthians 9:2). (i) It reflects influence to self. **The liberal soul shall be made fat: and he that watereth shall be watered also himself** (Proverbs 11:25). (j) It keeps back the devourer and makes the vine hold the fruit until the time. **And I will rebuke the devourer for your sakes, and he shall not destroy the fruits of your ground; neither shall your vine cast her fruit before the time in the field, saith the Lord of hosts** (Malachi 3:11). (k) It is a greater blessing than receiving. **I have shewed you all things, how that so labouring ye ought to support the weak, and to remember the words of the Lord Jesus, how he said, It is more blessed to give than to receive** (Acts 20:35). (l) It makes the ground give its increase and heaven its dew. **For the seed shall be prosperous; the vine shall give her fruit, and the ground shall give her increase, and the heavens shall give** their dew; and I will cause the remnant of this people to possess all these things (Zechariah 8:12). (m) It fills our barns and places with plenty. **So shall thy barns be filled with plenty, and thy presses shall burst out with new wine** (Proverbs 3:10). (n) It proves sincere love. **Therefore, as ye abound in everything, in faith, and utterance, and knowledge, and in all diligence, and in your love to us, see that ye abound in this grace also. I speak not by commandment, but by occasion of the forwardness of others, and to prove the sincerity of your love** (2 Corinthians 8:7, 8). (o) Because we cannot carry it with us when we die. **For he seeth that wise men die, likewise the fool and the brutish person perish, and leave their wealth to others. Be not thou afraid when one is made rich, when the glory of his house is increased; for when he dieth he shall carry nothing away: his glory shall not descend after him** (Psalm 49:10, 16, 17). **But those riches perish by evil travail: and he begetteth a son, and there is nothing in his hand. As he came forth of his mother's womb, naked shall he return to go as he came, and shall take nothing of his labour, which he may carry away in his hand** (Ecclesiastes 5:14, 15). (p) We cannot tell who will get our wealth after we die, a wise man or a fool. **Surely every man walketh in a vain show: surely they are disquieted in vain: he heapeth up riches, and knoweth not who shall gather them** (Psalm 39:6). **Yea, I hated all my labour which I had taken under the sun: because I should leave it unto the man that shall be after me. And who knoweth whether he shall be a wise man or a fool? yet shall he have rule over all my labour wherein I have laboured, and wherein I have shewed myself wise under the sun. This is also vanity** (Ecclesiastes 2:18, 19). (q) It pays in the last judgment. For **I was an hungered, and ye gave me meat: I was thirsty, and ye gave me drink: I was a stranger, and ye took me in: Naked, and ye clothed me: I was sick, and ye visited me: I was in prison, and ye came unto me. Then shall the righteous answer him, saying, Lord, when saw we thee an hungred, and fed thee or thirsty, and gave thee drink. When saw we thee a stranger, and took thee in or naked, and clothed thee, Or when saw we thee sick, or in prison, and came unto thee? And the King shall answer and say unto them, Verily I say unto you, In-**

# CHRISTIAN GIVING, PAYING TITHES 103

asmuch as ye have done it unto one of the least of these my brethren, ye have done it unto me (Matthew 25:35-40).

## X. Results Of Not Giving

It brings destruction to that which one possesses. That which the palmerworm hath left hath the locust eaten; and that which the locust hath left hath the cankerworm eaten; and that which the cankerworm hath left hath the caterpillar eaten. The field is wasted, the land mourneth; for the corn is wasted: the new wine is dried up, the oil languisheth. Be ye ashamed, O ye husbandmen; howl, O ye vine dressers, for the wheat and for the barley; because the harvest of the field, is perished. The vine is dried up, and the fig tree languisheth; the pomegranate tree, the palm tree also, and the apple tree, even all the trees of the field, are withered: because joy is withered away from the sons of men. The seed is rotten under their clods, the garners are laid desolate, the barns are broken down; for the corn is withered. How do the beasts groan? the herds of cattle are perplexed, because they have no pleasure; yea, the flocks of sheep are made desolate. O Lord, to thee will I cry: for the fire hath devoured the pastures of the wilderness, and the flame hath burned all the trees of the field. The beasts of the field cry also unto thee: for the rivers of waters are dried up, and the fire hath devoured the pastures of the wilderness (Joel 1:4, 10-12, 17-20). Now therefore thus saith the Lord of hosts; Consider your ways. Ye have sown much, and bring in little; ye eat, but ye have not enough; ye drink, but ye are not filled with drink; ye clothe you, but there is none warm; and he that earneth wages earneth wages to put it into a bag with holes. Thus saith the Lord of hosts; Consider your ways. Go up to the mountain, and bring wood, and build the house; and I will take pleasure in it, and I will be glorified, saith the Lord. Ye looked for much, and, lo, it came to little; and when ye brought it home, I did blow upon it. Why? saith the Lord of hosts. Because of mine house that is waste, and ye run every man unto his own house. Therefore the heaven over you is stayed from dew, and the earth is stayed from her fruit. And I called for a drought upon the land, and upon the mountains, and upon the corn, and upon the new wine, and upon the oil, and upon that which the ground bringeth forth, and upon men, and upon cattle, and upon all the labour of the hands (Haggai 1:5-11).

www.ingramcontent.com/pod-product-compliance
Lightning Source LLC
Chambersburg PA
CBHW071305040426
42444CB00009B/1884